Protocols
of
  Reading

Protocols

of

Reading

Robert
Scholes

YALE UNIVERSITY PRESS
NEW HAVEN AND LONDON

Title page illustration: *The Education of the Virgin*, attributed to
Georges de La Tour (1593–1652). Copyright The Frick Collection,
New York. Reprinted by permission.

*Designed by Nancy Ovedovitz and set in Galliard type by The Composing
Room of Michigan, Inc. Printed in the United States of America by Vail-
Ballou Press, Binghamton, New York.*

Library of Congress Cataloging-in-Publicaton Data

Scholes, Robert E.
    Protocols of reading / Robert Scholes.
        p. cm.
    Bibliography: p.
    Includes index.
    ISBN 0–300–04513–1 (alk. paper)
    1. Books and reading. 2. Criticism. I. Title.
Z1003.S3947 1989
028'.9—dc19   89–5588
                                                        CIP

*The paper in this book meets the guidelines for permanence and durability
of the Committee on Production Guidelines for Book Longevity of the
Council on Library Resources.*

10 9 8 7 6 5 4 3 2 1

To Jo Ann Schott Putnam-Scholes

A whole life story in those names! I'm glad mine comes
last. What I have to say needs more eloquence than
comes easily in our own language, so I have borrowed
some words from our mutual friend, Mario
Cavaradossi:

Amaro sol per te m'era il morire,
Da te la vita prende ogni splendore,
All'esser mio la gioa ed il desire
Nascondi te, come di fiamma ardore.
Io folgorare i cieli e scolorire
Vedrò nell'ochio tuo rivelatore,
E la beltà delle cose più mire
Avrà solo da te voce e colore.

Contents

Preface

"Protocols of Reading"—the phrase is Jacques Derrida's. He says we need them but he has never found any that satisfy him. This book is *not*, let me hasten to say, an attempt to provide a set that would please him. It is, rather, a meditation, an essay in three parts, on the subject of what reading is and what it ought to be. Among other things it is intended as a gesture of gratitude, an attempt to repay to reading—and to those whose texts I have read—some of what I owe for fifty years of pleasure and learning. It is also meant to provide a particular view of reading in the context of current debates on the subject. This view is informed by my own varied experiences as a reader, of course, but its formulation, as will be apparent, owes a good deal to recent semiotic thought, and in particular to the work of Roland Barthes and Umberto Eco. The view I present, it should also be acknowledged, is consciously and deliberately set against the deconstructive theory and practice of reading, which is examined and contested especially in chapters 2 and 3. Without deconstruction, it is fair to say, I would probably not have been driven to write this kind of book at the present time. I am grateful, then, to Jacques Derrida, in particular. To struggle with (or against) his views is in itself an education, a valuable reading experience.

In thinking about these matters I have followed, in a general way, the scheme outlined in *Textual Power,* in which reading, interpretation, and criticism were presented—admittedly, in a simple and schematic way—as dimensions or aspects of a larger process, which, to our confusion, we also usually call "reading." The notions of reading, interpretation, and criticism developed here are not exactly the same as those outlined in that earlier book, however, and the whole matter is presented in what I hope is a richer and more suggestive way. In particular, I have tried to function as a reader myself throughout this book, seeking to embody and illustrate my conclusions rather than to "prove" them. In this process I have deliberately drawn my examples from a wide range of texts in various media. Finally, I have not tried to hide behind some mask of scholarly objectivity in presenting these views. My own strong feelings about the uses and abuses of reading have driven the writing of this book, and I can only hope that the writing itself is in some way adequate to that originating impulse.

In the first chapter, I propose a semiotic theory of reading as an intertextual process governed by an active reader. In the second chapter I take up the question of protocols directly, exploring the tensions between our desire for certainty of interpretation and our recognition that such certainty is not possible. And in the third chapter, under the heading of "criticism," I consider the relation between the texts we read and the world in which we act and suffer—a relationship which is itself textualized in the tension among the aesthetic, the rhetorical, and the ethical dimensions of the reading process. Animating this final chapter, as indeed the whole of the book, is my belief that reading, though it may be a kind of action, is not the whole action but a part of it, remaining incomplete unless and until it is absorbed and transformed in the thoughts and deeds of readers. I believe that reading can and should answer to social and ethical concerns.

I have already acknowledged some large intellectual debts. I must also mention here, with pleasure, my gratitude for specific instances of advice, assistance, encouragement, criticism, and provocation from a number of people—none of whom must be blamed for the results. I won't say who did what. They know who they are—especially the provocateurs. They are, alphabetically, Shari Benstock, Gerald

Bruns, Arthur Danto, Diana Fuss, Jonathan Goldberg, Annie Goldson, Gerald Graff, Paul Hernadi, William Keach, Frank Kermode, Carl Klaus, George Levine, Kim Merker, Robert Robertson, Naomi Schor, Kaja Silverman, Michael Silverman, Theodore Sizer, Leslie Thornton, Elizabeth Weed, and Hayden White. In particular, I want to thank my colleague Albert Cook for perceptive, rapid, and tough readings of some early drafts of this material, and my collaborators Nancy Comley and Gregory Ulmer for what our work on *Text Book* has contributed to these pages. In the final stages of production I was fortunate to work with Elizabeth Casey, a copy editor who sees beyond the letter of a text. I am especially grateful to her and to Ellen Graham, who has been critically supportive over the years. Russell Potter prepared the index and Caroline Murphy saw the book through the press. My thanks to them both. Early versions of this material appeared in *Critical Inquiry*, *Novel*, and Alice Jardine and Paul Smith's *Men in Feminism*. The manuscript was completed during sabbatic leave from Brown University. Without which, not.

One

Reading:
An Intertextual
Activity

And no doubt that is what reading is: rewriting the text of the work within the text of our lives.

Roland Barthes

hough this whole book will be an attempt to say what reading is and what it should be, I cannot begin without proposing some preliminary notion of reading, however inadequate it may prove to be in the long run. In our ordinary speech acts we mention reading all the time. We say that we read books and maga zines and newspapers, to be sure, but we also speak of trying to read a person's expression or motives, and it is common, for instance, to speak of a quarterback or defensive captain on a football team trying to read the alignment opposing him. We read music, of course, and other forms of nonverbal notation, such as maps and choreography. Astrologers claim to read the stars—which astronomers also read, but according to a different code. We do not, in ordinary parlance, say that we read films or television (we "view" or "watch" them), though semioticians read—or say they read—such texts all the time. I shall be making—and trying to justify, here—the semiotic assumption that all the world's a text, which is very close to what Jacques Derrida said in his famous (now, perhaps, infamous) statement about there being nothing outside textuality.

This statement, as Derrida himself has found it necessary to explain, does not mean that there is no difference between what I may write about you in a book and what you are in reality. It only means that neither you nor I have access to the real you outside of reading. Each of us gets signs of himself or herself, messages from the nervous system, for example, which we learn to read. By such reading we construct ourselves for ourselves, as intelligible entities: as texts. We perceive one another, as well, through signs. Some signs, of course, convey more information than others, or better information, and one of the great problems for the theory and practice of reading is what we might mean by "better" in such cases. We shall be returning to this problem again and again in the following pages. We shall also take up more than once, from more than one angle, the question of whether there is any method of right reading that can be learned or taught. The possibility of rules or protocols of reading is acknowledged in the title of this book, but I should say at once that I have no simple system to propose. Reading is indeed learned and taught; it is done well and done badly; but it has too much in it of art and craft to yield entirely— or even largely—to methodization. Still, education amounts to taking method as far as it will go and then finding some way to go a bit further without it. Just that shall be my enterprise, which should be delayed no longer by pretextual maneuvers.

Let us read a picture—a picture of reading. In the front of this book is reproduced a painting in which we "see" two figures. Actually, this "seeing" is a reading, a decoding, in which we begin with interpretive gestures so apparently simple and natural that we think of them as "seeing," but we end by becoming more aware of our own share in constructing this visual text, as we bring more and more information from our other reading, from our experience of art, from our lives, to bear upon this process. We begin, then, by seeing two figures, a woman holding a book from which a child, apparently a girl, is reading, with the aid of a large candle that the girl holds in her left hand. The candle, sole source of light in the picture, connects the shining pages of the book to the bright, pale face of the girl. The painter has been very attentive to the play of light and shadow caused by the candle, in particular representing with great care the way the light comes around and through the right hand of the girl, which is raised in a gesture that is vaguely familiar, directly between the candle flame and our view of that flame. This positioning of the hand indicates the painter's awareness of us, the readers of this painted text, gazing out of the shadows at these two figures. It is the painter who has put the hand where it is, put us into this shadow. Opposite us, on a table at the back of this dark room, lies a wicker basket not so different from the laundry baskets we use today. The candlelight glows on this object and projects a shadowy image of it on the dark wall behind it. This is, then, a painting that is about reading, the activity represented in it, and about seeing, about light and shadow.

Looking more closely at the human beings represented in the painting, as we naturally do, we can seen that the woman holding the book for the girl is watching her with half-closed eyes, an expression on her face that is hard to read, except that it suggests calm and patience. It might be the expression of a teacher. The woman holds the book with her thumbs in the margins, so as not to obscure the text: her right thumb firmly placed, her left at the very edge of the right-hand page of the book, as if ready for it to be turned over. The girl, who is serious if not solemn, has her lips just slightly parted, as if she is reading or about to read this text aloud. Both woman and child appear plainly but comfortably dressed, in the garments of another time than ours, another place than ours. They are in a house, a domestic space, and they are represented in a manner that is the essence of simplicity and tranquility. The picture is in the manner of Georges de La Tour, who painted in Lorraine, in the northeastern corner of France, during the first half of the seventeenth century. There are several others like it— all, apparently, copies of one or more lost originals by La Tour himself. Several of them, including this one, bear the same title, *The Education of the Virgin*. Awareness of these few words will complicate and enrich our reading of this text.

From the Middle Ages to La Tour's time many artists represented scenes from the life of Mary—but not this scene. In the Annunciation, painted over and over again by medieval and Renaissance artists, and so it came to pass, beginning, apparently, in some Books of Hours and culminating in this painting of La Tour's.

If we read this painting in the light of its title it becomes a richer, more fruitful text. It also becomes more problematic. Like the candle which reveals the network or *textum* of the basket so plainly to us, but also offers us two or more ghostly handles for a basket which presents only one to our direct vision, the title also throws a textual shadow on the wall. If this is Mary at her reading lessons, our desire for narrative completeness drives us to seek a similar level of specificity for the other details of the text. We are driven to name the teacher as her mother, St. Anne, and to wonder what can be the book that she is reading aloud so seriously. We also, seeing her as the future mother of Jesus, now see in that curious gesture of her right hand a pose familiar to us from many paintings of Christ himself and the saints. This is the hieratic sign that accompanies miracles and revelations, when the Truth is uttered or revealed in action. It is also, of course, a shielding of the flame of a candle, a reflector of flesh that perhaps enhances the light on the text. But what text is this? What is she reading?

To answer this question, we must consider more carefully exactly where—and when—we are in this painting. If this is indeed Mary at her lessons, we are in a biblical time and space. But the clothing and the form of the book itself suggest a time and place nearer to that of La Tour himself. These may well be members of his own household, wearing their customary clothing in the year 1648 or thereabouts, holding a candle such as they customarily used to light their house, in front of their own laundry basket. The basket itself, and the domestic quality of this quiet scene, links the painting to the genre painters of

Mary might be people very different from those of Lorraine, living in surroundings that would have little in common with these. Everything works the other way here. This is a naturalism that is innocent of historicism. Mary and her mother display no halos here. In this northern culture the iconography of Catholic painting is domesticated, made plainer, more pure. If the light in this painting shows the heritage of Caravaggio, the simplicity and repose of the figures comes from another direction. The combination of these represents La Tour's special vision, which has proved of such interest in the present century that this painting of doubtful attribution hangs in the Frick Collection, on the same wall as some of the finest work of Rembrandt and Vermeer. No one knows who painted it, but no one questions that La Tour's vision has shaped this visual text.

The serenity and specificity of this vision, as I have suggested, draw the reader of this painted text into an active process that involves a mixture of research and imagination. We actively seek contextual information and we also seek to enter the world of the painting and name the objects we have constructed from the clues upon the painted surface. Above all, our eyes are drawn to that book, gleaming so brightly in the center of light. What book would be the major text for the instruction of the future Mother of God? We cannot read a word of it (and in the attempt I have got so close as to invite the attention of a museum guard). It is not a book for us, but only the sign of a book, as the people we "see" in the painting are only signs that we read as people. We cannot enter the world of this or any other painting. The reader is always outside the text. This is one of the things that it means to be a reader—to be outside. The price of entry is the labor of production itself. To read rightly we must start to write ourselves. We shall have to add something to this text in order to read it. In the present case, we can name the book Mary reads only by accepting the responsibility for a reading that is "ours"—and this is precisely what we should do. Let us say that she is reading a Bible.

The child is reading a Bible, let us say, because this is the right thing for her to be reading. It was a frequent text of instruction in La Tour's time and a very appropriate one. In the education of the Virgin, the Bible is a very important text for Mary to know, because her role is prefigured in it in prophetic language, even if what she reads is only the Old Testament. If this painted text were historically imagined, of course, the Jewish Law would be all the Bible that a child could read—but, as we have seen, this is not a text historically imagined. This is a text in which Mary and her mother are seen as contemporaries of the painter. It may well be that *this* Mary is reading a text that includes both Old and New Testaments. In short, she may well be reading her own story, the book of herself. Fanciful, you will say, or impossible. Impossible, yes, I would say, but likely all the same. For this is an allegory of reading. This is what we all do, all the time, when we read, and what we should do. To read at all, we must read the book of ourselves in the texts in front of us, and we must bring the text home, into our thoughts and lives, into our judgments and deeds. We cannot enter the texts we read, but they can enter us. That is what reading is all about. And that is why we should read this painting about reading in the way that we have just read it. Such reading involves looking closely at the text (so closely, perhaps, as to alarm its protectors); it also involves situating the text, learning about it, seeing it among others of its kind; and, first and last, reading requires us to make the text our own in thought, word, and deed, like the young Mary reading the Bible: seriously thoughtful, saying the words aloud, preparing to live the life to which the text directs her.

I have accepted the Derridean principle that there is no outside to textuality, but I have also said that the reader is always outside the text. This looks like confusion at worst and paradox at best, but it is neither. We are always outside any particular text we may attempt to read. This is why interpretation is a problem for us. But we are never outside the whole web of textuality in which we hold our cultural being and in which every text awakens echoes and harmonies. Every text that comes to us comes from before our moment in time, but each text can be read only by connecting it to the unfinished work of textuality. To read is to face the past, to accept what has happened as, in the words of L. P. Hartley, happening in "another country," where "they do things differently." Much as we might wish it, we cannot go *there*. To write, however, is to see world and text as unfinished, changeable. What we read is the past. What we write is the future. But we can write only with what we have read, and we can read only by writing. What I am suggesting is that we recognize our situation in a textual world that is always being written, that we can never quite read because we can never get outside it. Our ability to deal with this situation depends upon the quality of our always incomplete readings of all sorts of texts, but it also depends upon our ability to accept this incompleteness and to cherish the writing that informs all good reading, that is in fact the animating principle that keeps reading alive in a world that is not timeless but shaped and driven by time. To read is to write is to live is to read is to write "a long the riverrun past Eve and Adam's"—as long as we can go on.

Reading has two faces, looks in two directions. One direction is back, toward the source and original context of the signs we are deciphering. The other direction is forward, based on the textual situation of the person doing the reading. It is because reading is almost always an affair of at least two times, two places, and two consciousnesses that interpretation is the endlessly fascinating, difficult, and important matter that is. We see this most acutely in religious, legal, and literary reading, of course, but it is part of the fabric, of the structure, of reading as a human act, whatever is being read. Most theories of reading emphasize or privilege one face or the other of this two-faced activity. Reactionary theories emphasize the face that looks back. They tend to seek original truth or original intent as the master protocol of readings that will be as positive and unchanging as they can be. Radical theories emphasize the face that looks forward, insisting on the freedom and creativity of the reader along with the mutability of meanings in general.

Actually, the metaphor of faces looking forward and backward is itself a way of reading—a method of interpreting the process of reading that is the object of our attention here. As such, this metaphor clarifies a complex situation by simplifying it, but it also obscures the situation by that very simplification. One way to interpret the process of reading more adequately will be to find a metaphor that simplifies less brutally. The trouble with backward and forward as a descriptive metaphor is that it is one-dimensional, like a point moving along a single line. A metaphor that is two-dimensional may enable us to clarify a complex system in a more adequate manner. In the present case, we will probably do better to think of reading in terms of centripetal and centrifugal postures. Centripetal reading conceives of a text in terms of an original intention located at the center of that text. Reading done under this rubric will try to reduce the text to this pure core of unmixed intentionality. Centrifugal reading, on the other hand, sees the life of a text as occurring along its circumference, which is constantly expanding, encompassing new possibilities of meaning. The paired notions of centrifugality and centripetality constitute a "better" metaphor for reading than backward- and forward-looking, I would say, because two-dimensional geometry is a lot more supple than one-dimensional geometry. A circle is a figure almost as clear as a straight line, but it covers a lot more territory. In this case, the notions of closing in and opening out also manage to catch up some of the ways in which we have regularly thought about the two attitudes toward reading that I am trying to describe. But this is still a two-term or binary system, all too easily shifted into an invidious polarity of centrist conservatives and marginal radicals, reducers and expanders, truth seekers and sophists, or what you will.

Both these metaphors, the line and the circle, then, are aids to thought at first but finally become obstacles that must be discarded. To the extent that we have been "reading" the situation of reading itself, this process of inventing interpretive metaphors and then abandoning them should have a good deal of explanatory value for us. If this is the way we read—or one of the ways that we read—then reading is a creative process in which we generate, use, and discard our own texts as a way of making sense of the text we are ostensibly "reading." Reading, it cannot be emphasized too much, takes place in time. It is not just a matter of finding the "best" metaphor or other figure to understand a complex text, it is a matter of moving through a series of figures that enable us to understand our textual object better. In short, reading is a process—but not just any kind of process.

Reading, I shall argue, is dialectical. What I first called backward and forward movements and then centripetal and centrifugal impulses are the differential forces that drive the reading process. Without both of them, the process stops, becomes dead, ceases to be. And both of these forces or impulses, it must be emphasized, require creative and critical textual skills. We must resist the impulse to think of the centripetal as the uncreative, the unimaginative, the oppressive restriction of meaning. Even Derrida's metaphor of "respectful" reading as an indispensable guardrail keeping creative exorbitance on the road gives too little credit to the imaginative power required to construct such a guardrail in the first place and gives credit too readily to the centrifugal or exorbitant aspect of reading. My critical reading of Derrida, in this instance, requires that I understand his metaphor and find it inadequate or misleading with respect to its own object. Even to accomplish this little thing, I must read him centripetally and centrifugally. That is, I must seek his intent in the metaphor he uses and I must measure that metaphor alongside my own.

Reading is always, at once, the effort to comprehend and the effort to incorporate. I must invent the author, invent his or her intentions, using the evidence I can find to stimulate my creative process (a stimulation achieved in part by offering restrictions on that process, to be sure). I must also incorporate the text I am reading in my own textual repertory—a process that is not so much like putting a book on a shelf as like wiring in a new component in an electronic system, where connections must be made in the right places. In the present chapter I shall be concentrating on the second of these two dimensions of the reading process more visibly than on the first, partly because the first has received so much more attention from hermeneutic studies in general. Nevertheless, though I shall concentrate on how we connect texts to our own systems, I shall try to be constantly aware of the need to understand every text in its own terms in order to make such connections. What I mean by both understanding and connection are illustrated well in a short anecdote recounted by Roland Barthes:

The other evening I saw my first performance by a great dancer— preceded, among my friends, by a reputation of genius. The first ballet was danced by a young man whom I regarded as quite ordinary. "That can't be him," I said to myself with some assurance: stars never come on at the beginning and, besides, his entrance would have been applauded. In the intermission a friend enlightened me: of course it was Nureyev I had been watching. I was astonished; but during the second ballet my eyes were opened and I saw how incomparable this dancer's quality was and that he justified the ovation of an electrified house. Then I realized that I had just reproduced in 1978 the scene where the Proustian Narrator goes to see Berma act. Everything was there, quite literally: the longing, the murmurs, the expectation, the disappointment, the conversion, the movements of the audience. I left the theatre amazed by the genius . . . of Proust: we never stop adding to the "Search" (as Proust kept adding to his manuscripts), we never stop writing it. And no doubt that is what reading is: rewriting the text of the work within the text of our lives. [101]

There is no better definition of what I have been calling the centrifugal dimension of reading than that presented in the last sentence of Barthes's text—but, of course, Barthes's definition shows up the inadequacy of my metaphor (his text reads mine, critically) by making it clear that in this kind of reading there is a new center, the reader's own self, around which a new text is always being written. The centrifugal is always becoming centripetal again, just as reading is always a "rewriting the text of the work within the text of our lives." But let us read Barthes's text more carefully. He writes about an episode in his own life, a visit to the ballet in 1978, in which he has an experience that he discovers he has already read about in a novel. The experience, then, is not just his own, but a human experience that is "iterable" or repeatable just as words and thoughts are repeatable, never exactly the same, always changed by context, but never unique, either. If they were unique they would be like a totally strange word: unintelligible. We make sense of our lives as we make sense of any text, by accommodating new instances to old structures of meaning and experience.

A literary text like Proust's unfinished *Search for Lost Time* is important to us because it can enter the textual web that constitutes each of its readers and play a role in that reader's construction of his or her own narrative, the text we each make that convinces us we are living a "life." As Barthes points out, Proust kept revising his written text—a process that is continued by each reader for whom that novel is alive in memory, helping to shape and interpret new experiences. In a similar way, of course, Barthes is alive in my text and my thoughts, having become a part of what I think of as "me." Reading consists of bringing texts together. It is a constructive activity, a kind of writing. The texts

Barthes brings together are drawn, on the one hand, from his literary repertory, and, on the other, from his personal experience. Sometimes, this is how we read. But other times we may bring together two texts from personal memory, or two from books, or one from visual art and one from music—or any kind of textual combination. Such construction is pleasurable in itself, because it is that fundamental human action of making the world intelligible: in a word, reading. For the remainder of this chapter, I shall be looking at instances of reading as an intertextual activity, first in order to show that reading is indeed never just the reduction of a text to some kernel of predetermined intention but always the connecting of signs in one text to other signs altogether, and, second, in order to open the question of what makes for the best kinds of connections between texts—a question which, if it can be answered with any degree of satisfaction, may point to some protocols of reading after all.

Jacques Derrida has argued persuasively that perception itself is a kind of reading, in that we always perceive the signs of things rather than the things themselves. Yet, if perception is a kind of reading it is a rudimentary, preconscious kind, lacking precisely the deliberate, constructive element that is crucial to what I am calling reading here. Reading in this sense includes the elements of interpretation and criticism as well. Still, it is true that whatever can be perceived can be read, by subjecting our perceptions to a process of conscious contextualizing. We can and do read not only words and pictures but faces, clouds, waves, and even stones. Ruskin, for instance, tells us in *The Stones of Venice* that "the idea of reading a building as we would read Milton or Dante, and getting the same sort of delight out of the stones as out of the stanzas, never enters our mind for a moment" (166), but, of course, it had already entered one of our minds — namely, his—and for more than a moment, or he would not have been reading those stones and rewriting them for us at that very time, finding sermons in them, too, at every crack and cranny, and generally applying his own brand of textual varnish to everything in sight. Let us listen to him for a moment:

Her successor [Venice], like her [Tyre] in perfection of beauty, though less in endurance of dominion, is still left for our beholding in the final period of her decline: a ghost upon the sands of the sea, so weak—so quiet,—so bereft of all but her loveliness, that we might well doubt, as we watched her faint reflection in the mirage of the lagoon, which was the City, and which the Shadow.

I would endeavour to trace the lines of this image before it be forever lost, and to record, as far as I may, the warning which seems to me to be uttered by every one of the fast-gaining waves, that beat like passing bells, against the STONES OF VENICE. [Ruskin, 15]

Not only the stones, but the waves as well, talk to Ruskin, and the message they deliver is music to his ears, for they speak of a time when the stones will be gone and nothing but the text—and preeminently Ruskin's own text—will remain. I should say at once, perhaps, that I enjoy Ruskin's apocalyptic glee as I enjoy the stately and sensuous rhythms of his prose: words that beat like waves that beat like bells against the stones, da-dum, da-dum, only with elegant variations mitigating the iambic rumble. Irresistible, is it not? Yet something resists after all. In this case, we may say that Venice is what resists textualization by Ruskin.

Whatever uneasiness, whatever dis-satisfaction we may feel in reading Ruskin's words about the city, that very feeling marks the place where Venice hides. And it is this absence of Venice, in every text that seeks to read and transcribe the city, that generates the endless series of readings and writings in which Venice fails to materialize. Venice is an interesting case because the readings and writings of that city have been so extensive and have taken shape in so many media. The north portal of the facade of San Marco itself bears a representation of the saint's body being "translated" to San Marco. That is, there is a "reading" of San Marco as it was in the thirteenth century visible on the Basilica as it is now. In the Doge's Palace are paintings of the Doge's Palace. And so on. Modern writers have found the city no less fascinating than did their predecessors. Let us see what we can learn from the way two of them have tried to read and write the stones of Venice.

In September 1921 D. H. Lawrence wrote an acquaintance to the effect that he was working on a story about Venice, remarking that "Writing about Venice makes me realize how beautiful it is" (*Letters,*

662). The story may exist but has proved elusive. What we should notice about this comment, in any case, is that the writing precedes the beauty, causes the beauty to arise in the consciousness of the writer. Other texts cause other Venices to appear. In "Pomegranate," for instance, a poem he wrote at about the same time in his life, Lawrence calls Venice an "Abhorrent, green, slippery city" (*Poems*, 278), and in another poem, "St. Mark," he chronicles the metamorphosis of the lion of the senses into "a curly sheep-dog with dangerous propensities, / As Carpaccio will tell you" (324). The resulting "lion of the spirit," according to Lawrence, is the winged evangelistic lion of St. Mark, patron of this city:

Look at him, with his paw on the world
At Venice and elsewhere.
Going blind at last.

[325]

Lawrence apparently visited the city of "the curly sheep-dog" briefly, but the visit left few traces. In the record of his correspondence, we find plans to visit the city at various times, only one of which apparently materialized. It is true that at one time he contemplated writing a travel book about Venice, but ultimately he chose the more primitive Sardinia instead. Nevertheless, Venice was important to him as a text, a sign in a binary structure in which its meaning depended upon its contrast with America:

Italy consists of just one big arrangement of things to be admired. Every step you take, you get a church or a coliseum between your eyes, and down you have to go, on your knees in admiration. Down go the Americans, till Italy fairly trembles with the shock of their dropping knees. . . .

You can't fix a high water mark to human activity: not till you start to die. Here is Europe swimming in the stagnation of the ebb, congratulating itself on the long line of Cathedrals, Coliseums, Ghirlandajos which mark the horizon of the old high water: people swarming like the little crabs in the lagoons of Venice, in seas gone dead, and scuttling and gaping and pluming themselves conceitedly on the vision of St. Mark's and San Giorgio, looming up magic on the sky-and-water line beyond.

Alas for a people when its tradition is established, and its limit of beauty defined. Alas for a race which has an exhibition of modern paintings such as the one in the Gardens at Venice in this year of grace 1920. What is left but to look back to Tintoret? Let it look back then.

Let the beauty of Venice be a sort of zenith to us, beyond which there is no seeing. . . . We can do no more. We have reached our limits of beauty. But these are not the limits of all beauty. They are not the limit of all things: only of *us*.

Therefore St. Mark's need be no reproach to an American. It isn't *his* St. Mark's. It is ours. ["America, Listen to Your Own," *Phoenix*, 87–89]

Lawrence is guided by Ruskin, of course, in his feeling about Venice, but he is truly a modernist, and, unlike Ruskin, sees the end of European beauty as a prelude to the beginning of a new, perhaps more terrible, more barbaric dispensation in America. This is why Venice is positioned in *Lady Chatterley's Lover* precisely as the zenith beyond which there is no seeing, which Constance Chatterley visits at the end of her life as a "Lady." She never returns from there to Clifford, facing instead a future into which she can scarcely see but is willing to risk with Mellors. In Venice she can read the meaning of her old life more clearly than anywhere else, the city offering both its beauty and its decadence as a text for her to contemplate. It offers, for instance, the zenith of pleasure:

This was a holiday-place of all holiday places. The Lido, with its acres of sun-pinked or pyjamaed bodies, was like a strand with an endless heap of seals come up for mating. Too many people in the piazza, too many limbs and trunks of humanity on the Lido, too many gondolas, too many motor-launches, too many steamers, too many pigeons, too many ices, too many cocktails, too many men-servants wanting tips, too many languages rattling, too much, too much sun, too much smell of Venice, too many cargoes of strawberries, too many silk shawls, too many huge, raw-beef slices of water-melon on stalls: too much enjoyment, altogether far too much enjoyment. [242]

The images of the city, which have scarcely changed in the nearly seventy years since Lawrence saw it, become the signs of an excess of pleasure without substance. It is not so much wicked as wearying, all this enjoyment, and just a little ominous, like a carnival, a celebration of the flesh that is also a farewell, the end of something. Not only the epitome of excessive enjoyment, Venice is also for Connie Chatterley the incarnation of bourgeois capitalism: "Connie looked at Venice far off, low and rose-coloured upon the water. Built of money, blossomed of money, and dead with money. The money-deadness! Money, money, money, prostitution and deadness" (244). In these phrases Lawrence sounds a bit like another modernist who wrote of Venice, Ezra Pound. There is an ideology at work here that we shall try to "read" later in this chapter.

For Lawrence, Venice is a place that has lost its cultural function, lost what he calls its "living nodality." He contrasts it with Taos Pueblo, which "still remains its old nodality." In Venice, he says, "one feels the magic of the glamorous old node that once united East and West, but it is the beauty of an after-life" (*Phoenix*, 100). This is, of course, very close to Ruskin's view, but Lawrence cannot be bothered with Venice or by Venice as Ruskin was. It is another of Ruskin's followers, Marcel Proust, who most fully feels the attraction of the decadent old city on the lagoon. It is fair to say that Venice enters Lawrence's texts in a conventional way, largely coded for him in advance by Ruskin and simply adapted to reinforce his late turn away from Europe toward new possibilities in another hemisphere. For Proust, however, who went to school to Ruskin much more thoroughly and seriously than ever Lawrence did, Venice took on a significance that transcended Ruskin's apotheosis of the city's decadence and decline. Venice, like everything else in the *Recherche* becomes a Proustian place. If Lawrence could do no more than read Venice as Ruskin had already textualized it or rewrite it in a simple binarism opposed to Taos Pueblo and the New World, Proust deployed an imaginative power sufficient to transform the entire city and its vast lagoon into his very own cup of tea.

Venice exists in Proust's text in three modes: as anticipation, as actuality, and as recollection. The city's crucial textualization in this book is of course in the third mode, the search for a lost place epitomizing, as it does, the larger search for a lost time. You will recall that this scene comes in the last volume, when the narrator (we shall follow custom in calling him Marcel) is on his way to a reception at the house of the Princesse de Guermantes. He is at a low ebb intellectually and emotionally, believing that he has lost, perhaps forever, his ability to textualize both the world around him and the scenes of his past life. Only yesterday, in a spot culturally coded as "one of the most beautiful parts of France," he had found himself unable "to describe the line that separated sunlight from shadow on the tree trunks" (990). And today he fails when seeking to recall a comparable urban experience:

I now tried to bring out from the storehouse of my memory other "snapshots," particularly those I had "taken" in Venice, but just the word "snapshot" alone made it all as wearisome to me as an exhibition of photographs, and I felt within myself no more inclination or talent for describing now what I had seen several years before than I felt yesterday for describing what I was at that moment gazing upon with a painstaking and listless eye. [991]

This inability to describe needs to be analyzed a bit. It is precisely a failure of referential textuality, a crisis at the point where language and the world intersect, a simultaneous loss of the ability to read the world adequately and to write it. Marcel has begun to doubt whether words can give an adequate account of the world. He describes this as a loss of faith in his own talent or in the larger possibilities of literature itself: "now I had the proof that I was not good at anything, that I could no longer hope to find joy in literature, whether through my own fault, for lack of talent, or because literature itself was less pregnant with reality than I had thought." It is, of course, precisely a failure to describe Venice that brings on this episode, which is the climactic moment of the entire narrative. Venice, because it is the most textualized and textualizable of cities, becomes the measure of Marcel's failure—and the possible failure of literature itself.

At this very moment, as you will recall, startled by the sudden arrival of a car in the courtyard whose flagstones he is crossing, Marcel stumbles into a position that unlocks both his memories and his artistic talent. Sensing a vision not yet fully entered into his consciousness, he does a clumsy little dance in the courtyard, seeking to recover the sensation he had felt when he first stumbled. Finally he

glimpses it: "again the dazzling, elusive vision brushed me with its
wings. . . . And almost immediately I recognized it; it was Venice. . . .
But why had the mental images of Combray and Venice at their
respective moments given me a sense of joy like a sense of certainty,
sufficient, without other proofs, to make me indifferent to death?"
(992). On the answer to this question rests one of the major problems
of modernism. It is clear that for Lawrence as for Thomas Mann,
Venice is a text in which death is powerfully inscribed. Why should it
speak to Proust of joy, certainty, and, above all, indifference to death?
Part of the answer, I believe, is that Proust has a more rigorous and
subtle notion of textuality than does either Mann or Lawrence. His
Venice is not a signifier bound to a single complex of meanings, but a
sign capable of changing its meaning radically from text to text. Here,
Venice is equal to Combray. Not only are the stones in the Guermantes' court equivalent to the stones of Venice for the moment, but
they are also comparable to the madeleine, recalling Venice "in the
same way" as the herb tea had recalled the village of Marcel's youth A
second part of the answer, however, is that in certain crucial respects
Proust is not a modernist at all but a major figure of romantic aestheticism, whose conception of writing and of the world is not oriented
toward history or toward the future but back toward the roots of
modernism in Kantian transcendentalism. What has happened to
Marcel is explained in the following crucial passage:

> In truth the person within me who was at that moment enjoying this
> impression enjoyed in it the qualities it possessed which were common to
> both an earlier day and the present moment, qualities which were
> independent of all considerations of time; and this person came into play
> only when, by this process of identifying the past within the present, he
> could find himself in the only environment in which he could live and
> enjoy the essence of things, that is to say, entirely outside of time. [905]

This is emphatically not a dialectical view of time or of history. It is a
transcendental view. The search for a lost time ends in the only place
where it could end successfully, in that transcendental place that is no
place, outside of time, in the eternity of aestheticism, where all places
and times mingle on an equal footing. I do not think that we can

follow Proust to that place "outside of time"—nor do I believe he was able to sustain the feeling of being in such a position. Still, we can learn an important lesson from Marcel's recovery of the ability to textualize experience. What enables him to recover is the linking of two times. His body, by connecting the feeling of these stones under foot to those other stones or the taste of this herb tea to that other herb tea, begins for him what we can now understand as the process of reading, connecting one time to another, one place to another, one text to another through the figures of memory, which are the same as the figures of speech. We read, as we talk, write, and think, by connecting signs and weaving texts, using the figures of resemblance, contiguity, and causality to accomplish this work, these being, as David Hume noted in his *Enquiry Concerning Human Understanding* (Par. 19), "the only three principles of connexion among ideas." Proust reminds us, among other things, of the joy, the pleasure we take in making such connections. Reading is not just a means to other ends. It is one of the great rewards for the use of our capacities, a reason for living, an end in itself.

Like any art, craft, or sport, reading becomes more rewarding as we master its intricacies to higher degrees. As with these other activities, also, we may continue to improve as readers until age begins to weaken our powers, presenting us with signs of our inevitable end. This analogy, like all analogies, can only be taken so far, but the development and decline of our physical and mental powers is no mere analogy but a pattern that each of us must undergo in every aspect of life and in the whole of it. We humans are the animals who know that we shall die. We know that our lives are shaped like stories, with a beginning, a middle, and an end, and that the end is inevitable. Reading, I am contending, consists, among other things, in recognizing and facing the signs of this pattern, too. We read life as well as books, and the activity of reading is really a matter of working through signs and texts in order to comprehend more fully and powerfully not only whatever may be presented therein but also our own situations, both in their particularity and historicity and in their more durable and inevitable dimensions.

Even the happiest of textual endings is an end, a kind of death. We read knowing that our lives as readers of this particular text are limited and that each word moves us closer to the end. Though a narrative may urge us onward toward its conclusion with considerable force, there is something in us that resists. We may dearly wish to finish a particular story, to know how it comes out, to experience the joy, the catharsis, or whatever lies in wait for us at the end, but at the same time—and the more pleasure the book is giving us the more strongly we feel this—we don't want it to end. We want it to go on forever. But books, like lives, do not go on forever. True, we can read a book again, starting over as Plato believed souls might start over again in life, but it is also true, as Heraclitus might have said, that the same person never reads the same book twice.

If my description of reading is correct, then it follows that we should read in a certain way. We should, in fact, read so as to get the most out of each experience of reading. If a book or a story or any other text is like a little life, and if our reading actually uses up precious time in that other story we think of as our lives, then we should make the most of our reading just as we should make the most of our lives. Reading reminds us that every text ends with a blank page and that what we get from every text is precisely balanced by what we give. Our skill, our learning, and our commitment to the text will determine, for each of us, the kind of experience that text provides. Learning to read books —or pictures, or films —is not just a matter of acquiring information from texts, it is a matter of learning to read and write the texts of our lives. Reading, seen this way, is not merely an academic experience but a way of accepting the fact that our lives are of limited duration and that whatever satisfaction we may achieve in life must come through the strength of our engagement with what is around us. We do well to read our lives with the same intensity we develop from learning to read our texts. We all encounter certain experiences that seem to call for more than a superficial understanding.

Now, before turning again to the sort of text that we more usually consider worthy of deep reflection, I want to use a personal experience to illustrate what I mean by reading life. This experience took place some years ago, when I owned a small sailboat that was capable of taking me farther than I had ever sailed in such a boat before. On the occasion that I am proposing to "read," my wife and I had decided to sail from our home waters of Narragansett Bay to the islands of southern Massachusetts, arriving finally at Nantucket. On our first day we sailed across Mount Hope Bay and down the sheltered waters of the Sakonnet River toward Rhode Island Sound and the islands. At a certain point near the mouth of that river—and it is typical of this kind of experience that the point itself cannot be located exactly in time or space—we were aware that something had happened, but it took us some time to grasp what it was, and it has taken me even longer to develop a reading of that experience. Indeed, I am not finished with it yet.

What happened was not a great adventure nor a life-threatening experience, though we had some of those in later years. It was, in its way, a perfectly ordinary thing. The experience began with both of us becoming aware that something had happened. The wind was the same; the sky had not changed from its bright, sunny blue; we were not sinking, nor aground, nor suffering from any of the dozens of problems that can overtake a boat under way. But something had happened that made everything different, and this something went on happening, with us becoming more and more aware of it before we could put a name to it and bring it fully to consciousness. What had happened was a simple thing, really. We had sailed far enough down the river to begin to encounter the great ground swells that come from far out in the ocean and rise higher as the bottom underneath them begins to affect their progress. These swells were gentle but immensely powerful, and they raised and lowered our little boat with awesome ease. This was a rhythm very different from the fussy little waves that we were used to in the sheltered waters where we regularly sailed. This was the ocean itself sending us a message that we could sense deep in our bodies, a message as ancient as the planet itself. It was a warning, of course, about the power of the winds that had made these waves and the sea that had carried that message so far, but it was more than a mere sign of danger. This rhythm whispered to us of primal things and we understood what it was saying. It was like returning to a state before birth and listening to your mother's heart beat, pumping life into your own arteries as well, for it spoke of life and death and said that they were one.

Writers far more eloquent than I have written of such things and their texts rushed into my head as I began to realize what I was experiencing. "She is our great sweet mother," says Buck Mulligan to Stephen Dedalus in the first chapter of *Ulysses*, standing on the parapet of their tower, looking out at the Irish Sea and quoting Swinburne. Those words and others came to my mind unbidden, as did my own experiences of the sea, from learning to ride the breakers as a child in the Atlantic Ocean to standing on the deck of a heavy cruiser in a Japanese harbor and looking at the massive ships thrown up on shoals and sea walls by a typhoon that we had ridden out with two anchors set and our engines turning slowly ahead. Often the sea is simply a reality that must be dealt with moment by moment or a toy that seems to exist for our pleasure alone, but this moment in the Sakonnet was a different kind of experience, one meant for reading, for bothering to understand. Such moments must be seized. When digested they become the very body of our consciousness, as the food we eat becomes our flesh.

Waves are not matter, they are energy or power incarnate, moving through matter in their own shape. I once asked a physicist why so many things came in the shape of waves. He said, "Because God likes waves." The wave is indeed a building block of our universe, something elemental if not eternal. We should bother to understand waves, then, especially when they come to us as messengers. Waves, of course, have been rippling through this chapter for some time. We observed Ruskin reading the waves of the Venice lagoon, for instance, and Lawrence drawing from the sea his metaphor of "Europe swimming in the stagnation of the ebb, congratulating itself on the long line of Cathedrals, Coliseums, Ghirlandajos which mark the horizon of the old high water: people swarming like the little crabs in the lagoons of Venice, in seas gone dead." Reading the waves of the Sakonnet River is largely a matter of connecting them to other waves, from books, pictures, and experience, already textualized in memory. To read is, among other things, to sort through this file of connected signs so as to place the new text in its proper relation to the old ones. These waves then move in memory, like the clouds in Auden's "Look, Stranger" that "pass the harbour mirror / And all the summer through the water saunter," from whence they may be summoned up, for instance, to play their part in the reading of a poem like W. S. Merwin's "Coming to the Morning," which connects waves and memory itself, beginning this way, " You make me remember all of the elements / the sea remembering all of its waves." Among other things, Merwin's poem suggests why it is that waves can communicate to us. As we read this wave-poem, we see such things as "the shape of one mountain" and we find that "our ears / are formed of the sea as we listen" (37). A poem like this, it seems to me, will be read best by being brought together with the traces of other texts in our memories. Like "the sea remembering all of its waves," we remember our own waves in order to read Merwin's. By such weavings of waves we actively shape the text that is our consciousness. As we link our readings, we write ourselves: "and our ears / are formed of the sea as we listen."

In selecting the illustrative material for this chapter I found myself enmeshed in the very textual process I am describing. Seeking a painting of the act of reading, I was led down paths of memory to *The Education of the Virgin*, which I later discovered to be connected by an extraordinary web of similarities and contrasts to a visual image I had already discussed in my manuscript: a photograph taken by the American photographer W. Eugene Smith in Japan in 1972. Across three hundred years and more, across all the cultural differences that divide East from West, across all the waves of the world, these two visual images speak to one another in my book because they are part of the textual network out of which my own consciousness is woven. In both images mothers look at daughters, but the futures of those daughters, already written, though in different codes, are themselves terribly different. Let us begin to read this second image.

The picture is called *Tomoko in the Bath*. It is a powerful, disturbing picture even in our first, hasty glance at it, but we need to read it in order to come to grips with the sources of this power and to turn our first reactions into something more focused, more deliberate, more aware, and closer to action, but also more detached and contemplative and closer to full understanding. What we see, and it is not easy to contemplate, is a humanoid creature stretched out diagonally across a square primitive bath tub, naked and supported by another person, also in the tub, who is gazing at the misshapen face of the creature in

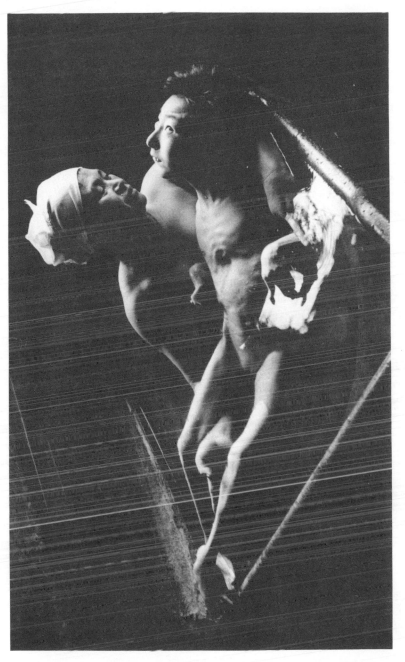

W. Eugene Smith, *Tomoko in the Bath*. Copyright © 1975 by Aileen and W. Eugene Smith. By permission of the photographer and Black Star.

the foreground. To make even the simplest kind of sense of this
picture we need more information than we can glean from the text
itself, though, as I said, we need nothing to be disturbed by the image
itself. This initial disturbance, I believe, comes from our reading of the
figure stretched out in the tub against some mental template we hold
of the human form. We can assign this creature to no species other
than our own, but we know that no human being ought to look like
that. Like us, it has arms and legs, but the legs are as thin as sticks and
the arms and hands are twisted into impossible shapes. Like us, it has a
torso, but this torso has ridges and lumps and whorls on it that no
human body ought to have. If it is human, it must have a sex. Naked
and exposed as it is, it offers our eyes the information about gender
that we inevitably seek. And so our gaze travels to the spot which
seems to tell us that this humanoid being is female. Nothing but the
genitals themselves on this poor body would have conveyed that
information.

   We could go on reading the image itself but already we have seen
too much to be satisfied with this inner text alone. What we have seen
drives us with great intensity to seek more information. We want to
know what this is, where it is, what has done this. In its original
context of publication, this information would have been readily
available. The picture was part of a book by the American photographer W. Eugene Smith, a photo essay on a Japanese fishing
village which first appeared in *Life* magazine in 1972. Some Japanese
friends had brought Smith to Minimata in the early 1970s, where he
found not only a village where fishing was done in traditional ways
but a place that had been ravaged by industrial pollution, which by
1956 had reached epidemic proportions. Smith lived in the village for
some time, eating the local food and getting to know the people, in his
own words, "as neighbors and friends." There he saw, and inevitably
photographed, the victims of mercury poisoning from factory wastes
in the area. These photographs, published in Japan as well as in the
United States, played a major role in the struggle of these people
against the Chisso Corporation and its pollution. In an interview
some years later Smith was asked about the picture we are trying to
read:

How did the famous picture of the mother washing her daughter come about?

By that process of getting to know the individuals. We looked after the child at times when the parents were on protests. They lived about a ten-minute walk from our house. Every time we went by the house, we would see that someone was always caring for her. I would see the wonderful love that the mother gave. She was always cheerful, and the more I watched, the more it seemed to me that it was a summation of the most beautiful aspects of courage that people were showing in Minimata in fighting the company and the government. Now this is called romanticism. But it was courage that I was interested in. Courage is romantic, too. I wanted somehow to symbolize the best, the strongest element of Minimata.

One day, I said to Aileen, my wife, "Let's try to make that photograph." I imagined a picture in which a child was being held by the mother and the love was coming through. I went to the house, tried very clumsily to explain to the mother that I wanted to show a picture in which Tomoko was naked so we could see what had happened to her body. I wanted to show her caring for the child. And she said, "Yes, I'm just about to give Tomoko her bath. Maybe that will help you." She first held the child on the outside of the bath and washed her as the Japanese do; then she put her into the bath. And I could see the picture building into what I was trying to say. I found it emotionally moving, and I found it very difficult to photograph through my tears. However, I made that photograph. It's as romantic as could be.

The photographer's information helps us both to place and to read the picture. The picture, we learn, is firmly and terribly grounded in history. It is a document that figured powerfully in convincing people in Japan and the rest of the world about the real threat of industrial pollution. As a document, it is part of a chain of cause-and-effect reasoning, linking the practices of a particular industry to this and other instances of human anguish and deformation. It has functioned with great effectiveness as a work of agitation and propaganda. It would be a serious error to read the picture as if it were not grounded in this history or to forget the need for a continuing struggle to protect ourselves and our planet from the vast carelessness of a "market economy" that is reckless of ecology. It would also, however, be an error to read it only in this way. Reading the photographer's words (which must themselves, of course, be interpreted), we learn that he is somewhat embarrassed by the power of his image to manipulate emotion. He hides behind the word *romantic*, pleading guilty to romanticism, perhaps, so as not to be charged with sentimentality. What he tells us helps to put the picture into its proper political context, as a document in a political and economic struggle of the victims of pollution against a large corporation backed by a national government. This context helps to explain how and why he was permitted to achieve the intimacy required for the picture to be taken. His discussion also helps us to understand some other important aspects of the picture. His concept and his message preceded the image itself. "I could see the picture building into what I was trying to say," he tells us. Learning to read visual images is partly a matter of understanding how the visual and conceptual are linked in consciousness. In this case, I should like to suggest, Smith knew what he was looking for because he knew one of the most persistent and elaborate linkages of image and concept in our cultural history: the iconographic code of the *pietà*: the image of the *mater dolorosa*, holding in her arms the mutilated body of her crucified child. What Smith experienced as "the picture building" was in fact the movement of the bodies of mother and child toward this already coded icon.

Those of us brought up in the tradition of Christian art read the picture, unconsciously, in terms of this cultural code, which conditions our response. No matter that those involved are Japanese; the photographer was not. To read this image consciously, in the manner I have been deploying under the rubric of "bothering" to read, is to perceive both the icon and the image: to react, and to know why we react as we do. We also, as I have already indicated, react powerfully to the terrible deformation of Tomoko's body, but this deformation is also coded, to some extent, by our familiarity with artistic presentations of the norms of beauty, of what a body ought to look like. To see this image, however, as the mere repetition of what has been already coded would be to trivialize it by denying its real power over us. Are we nothing but our codes? I think we are more, though it is not easy to say exactly what this "more" may be. We should at least consider what lies behind the power of the icons themselves, that is, where the story of Christ's passion and its visual representation get their power.

The expression of tenderness and love on the face of Tomoko's mother speaks to us of what lies behind the icons themselves: a human reality which, if it isn't eternal, nevertheless transcends the real differences between Eastern and Western culture. "*Amor matris*," thinks Stephen Dedalus as he tutors the hapless Cyril Sargent, "subjective and objective genetive." Looking at Sargent, Stephen muses, "Ugly and futile: lean neck and tangled hair and a stain of ink, a snail's bed. Yet someone had loved him, borne him in her arms and in her heart. But for her the race of the world would have trampled him under foot, a squashed boneless snail. She had loved his weak and watery blood drained from her own. Was that then real? the only true thing in life?" (Joyce, *Ulysses*, 23). Joyce's and Smith's texts read each other, speak to each other, and we read them more richly through one another and through the texts of our lives. I can remember my own father saying in his teasing manner that I had a face that only a mother could love. A man who drew his wisdom from a patchy schooling supplemented by the literature of music halls and sports pages, he often spoke out of a cultural doxology that lent his jokes a certain gravity. Smith's picture reminds me of his words, puts even me in that terrible picture. Many of us, if truly seen, might look so misshapen. And where shall we get that kind of love?

Reading is not just a matter of standing safely outside texts, where their power cannot reach us. It is a matter of entering, of passing through the looking glass and seeing ourselves on the other side. If Derrida is right, and on this question I think he is, there is no place for us to stand outside of textuality, anyway. When we become aware of ourselves, we are already thoroughly developed as textual creatures. What we are and what we may become are already shaped by powerful cultural texts. In my own reading of Smith's photograph, for instance, I can find traces of a Roman Catholic ideology that I have explicitly rejected but cannot quite eliminate from my consciousness. We cannot start ourselves over as blank pages but must go on writing the texts of ourselves from where we find ourselves to be. In the final section of this chapter, I propose to look further into this matter of the cultural construction of human subjectivity. In particular, I am interested in how we may read or bring to light deep ideological structures that manifest themselves only in patterns that appear in the lives of different individuals and in the supposedly unique cultural objects that such individuals produce.

Such a reading of ideology can only be performed in a tentative manner, and very much under the sign of the hermeneutic circle. That is, the reader must postulate some ideological structure, derived by an inductive (or abductive) leap, then read the lives and texts in question in the light of that structure, hoping to confirm or modify the initial postulation. Among other things, I shall be trying to develop and demonstrate a method for this kind of reading, in which an ideological structure is initially described in terms of simple binarisms that may be refined under the pressure of concrete examples. My examples will be several exceptional young men born in Europe in time to participate fully in the cultural processes of modernism. The single example examined in the fullest detail will be James Joyce, about whose intellectual development during certain crucial years we have sufficient data to observe, at least occasionally, the workings of ideology at the microstructural level. (The absence of women from this brief consideration should be noted. A preliminary investigation has led me to believe that women experienced the ideology of modernism in somewhat different ways from men, for the most part—or perhaps experienced a different ideology. The subject is complex and fascinating. I hope to produce a study of women in modernism at some time in the future. My present method, however, will be to read the lives of several young as texts constructed within the ideology of European modernism.) Each of these lives can be read (or written) as a unique story. But the lives of these very different people can also be seen as startlingly similar despite their enormous differences, as if there were a master narrative for that culture, from which many individual lives took their departure. The lives I shall examine are those of exceptional people, to be sure, who were especially interested in politics or the arts, or both, and who made some impact on the culture that had shaped them. Nevertheless, their lives fit easily within a single paradigm, which offers us a key to the reading of modernism itself as a historical phenomenon. The paradigm or master narrative goes this way:

Many talented young people born in Europe in the 1880s came under the spell of an idealistic socialism that was international in its aspirations and grounded upon sympathy for the working class, combined with a powerful dislike of the bourgeoisie and its institutions. As the extreme difficulty—perhaps the impossibility—of achieving the socialist program became apparent, these individuals shifted their goals in various directions, all of which were marked by certain authoritarian and totalizing proclivities. In the case of James Joyce, who will be my central example here, these proclivities took an aesthetic direction, toward the artist as a supreme figure, absolute in his own world and without any specific social responsibility. Other talented young men, who had contemplated literary careers, turned from international socialism toward more authoritarian political forms: toward nationalism, fascism, or the authoritarian "socialism in one country" that came to be known as Stalinism. My major point is that a certain disillusionment with the possibilities of international socialism led young men of great talent toward authoritarian solutions, whether in art, religion, or politics. Aesthetic modernism, then, like fascism and Stalinism, was given a powerful impetus by the failure of international socialism in the first several decades of the twentieth century.

To see James Joyce in terms of this paradigm, we must learn to take seriously his early interest in socialism. Before looking at this aspect of his life, however, we shall first have to construct a "reading" of his first two and a half decades, situating that reading at a level of abstraction that will enable us to connect his life to the lives of other young Europeans of his generation. Joyce was born in 1882, in the suburbs of a city, in a country on the fringe of Europe. His family was in financial difficulties, but they managed to send him to a religious boarding school and later to other schools run by the Catholic Church. He was a rather delicate child, much better at studies than at games, who sometimes rebelled against the school authorities and sometimes was honored by them. He had to leave his first school when his father lost his job. As he matured he alternated between fits of excessive piety and visits to Dublin's red-light district ("Nightown" in *Ulysses*). He was a talented singer and contemplated a musical career, once singing in a contest against the future star tenor, John McCormack. At the age of 18 he delivered a stirring address at University College, Dublin, in which he pleaded the cause of his dramatic idol, Henrik Ibsen. At that time he thought that he himself would be a dramatist of Ibsen's type.

In 1902 he graduated from college as a specialist in modern languages. He spent some time in Paris, intending to write a treatise on aesthetics. He was called home because his mother was dying, and this event caused him great personal anguish, since he was very fond of his mother but could no longer share her religious faith. He taught school for a while after her death, but had trouble keeping order. He was perpetually in debt and borrowed heavily from friends and casual acquaintances alike. In 1904 he left his native country with a woman he would marry decades later. They lived in Paris briefly that year but soon moved on and finally settled in the Italian-speaking part of Austria, where their first child was born. They moved briefly to Rome before returning to Trieste, where their second child was born. During these years they experienced grinding poverty and its attendant forms of humiliation. Joyce kept writing fiction and poetry at this time, but he also wrote journalistic pieces and translated some works he admired from English into Italian. These were the years during which Joyce was serious about socialism. His own financial difficulties were acute, leading him to frequent expressions of resentment against the bourgeois class he saw as enjoying unfair advantages over him and his family. This phase of his life seems to have ended some time before 1910, with a massive and drastic repudiation of socialism and a renewed commitment to a world of art in which he could reign supreme.

Joyce's aesthetic turn has been so thoroughly noted that his earlier attitude has often been ignored or obscured by his critics. One of my purposes in this reading of his life, then, will be to register more fully his earlier phase of social thought and commitment, but before turning to that task I feel it incumbent upon me to explain more fully the method I am employing to situate Joyce and the other exemplary figures of my text. This is necessary, I believe, because I am trying to work in an area that lies between traditional literary studies and the historical and social disciplines. My object here is neither Joyce himself nor history itself, but European culture at a certain moment, and, in particular, this culture as a mediating factor, a structure of possibilities that presented Joyce and others of his generation with pathways that were already organized in the form of axiological or binary structures of value and choice. Culture, of course, is never that simple, and this binarizing is partly a method adopted for analytical convenience. In other words, I am making sense of a complex text by simplifying it. In short I am "reading" culture. If this were only a matter of this reader's convenience, however, it would be unworthy of serious regard as a method. I wish to argue, however, that this is how we all perceive culture, that culture comes to us like a language, already organized in terms of certain powerful binarisms.

I shall be trying to read certain texts—poems, letters, and even life stories—as symptoms of the larger super-text that is culture. My assumption is that culture presents itself or imposes itself upon individuals in the form of a system of binary oppositions along which values and choices must flow. In the first decades of this century in Europe, one of the major oppositions structuring values and choices was that between a secular or materialist socialism, on the one hand, and a spiritual or transcendental religion on the other. The rejection of one of these polar opposites by any individual led directly toward the acceptance of the other, so that a move away from religion, for instance, was directed by the cultural system into a move toward socialism, and a move away from socialism was likely to take the form of a move toward religion (or possibly toward some other form of idealism or mysticism).

One of the major cultural events of this period was the development of a new alternative, a new opposite for international socialism in the form of an aesthetically organized secular religion: fascism or national socialism. Parallel to this event, in a structure of opposition and complicity that remains to be worked out, was the development of another aesthetically organized secular religion: the religion of high modernist art. For those disillusioned with international socialism, the path to fascism and the path to modernism lay open. We are not talking about rigid structures, of course, but about lines of filiation, cultural pathways by which an individual, in abandoning one view or attitude, would be led toward one or another of a limited set of alternatives. I cannot claim to have this view of culture fully worked out, but I am certain that seeing culture as a textual network organized by a set of related axiological structures or polarities will prove to be a fruitful method of study in the developing field of cultural criticism.

Returning to Joyce, one of the important mediators of his thought on a number of subjects in 1906 and 1907 was the Italian historian Guglielmo Ferrero, whose book *L'Europa giovane (Young Europe)* Joyce was reading in 1906. (It was listed as next to Mercredy's Map of Ireland on Shelf J, back, among his books in Trieste.) Joyce was much taken with Ferrero at this time, and in particular with this 1897 book, subtitled "studies and voyages in the countries of the north." In September of 1906, Joyce found a picture postcard of Ferrero in Rome and wrote to his brother about it:

By the way, talking of faces I will send you a picture postcard of Guglielmo Ferrero and you will admit there is some hope for me. You would think he was a terrified Y.M.C.A. man with an inaudible voice. He wears spectacles, is delicate-looking and, altogether, is the type you would expect to find in some quiet nook in the Coffee-Palace nibbling a bun hastily and apologetically between the hours of half-past twelve and one. [*Letters*, 159]

Among other things, these remarks suggest that Joyce saw some parallels between Ferrero and himself. But he was also taken with Ferrero's writing and thinking about modern European culture and politics.

One day in November of 1906 Joyce wrote to Stanislaus that he was thinking of beginning his story "Ulysses" but felt too oppressed with cares. In the next sentence he turned to Ferrero's observations on Jews and anti-Semitism, noting that "the most arrogant statement made by Israel so far, he says, not excluding the gospel of Jesus, is Marx's proclamation that socialism is the fulfillment of a natural law" (*Letters*, 190). In the reference to this letter in the index to Richard Ellmann's edition of the letters, what should be "Ferrero on Marx" unaccountably appears as "Ferrero on Mary." This tiny change, the Freudian slip of a pious compositor, no doubt, is effected by simply cutting off a bit of Marx's X (a bit off the bottom, so to speak), turning Marx into Mary with a minimum of fuss. I read this error as symbolic of the tension between religion and socialism that constituted one of the structuring polarities of modernist ideology. This equation of X and Y is not a random event but an axiological error, the substitution of one ideology for its opposite. The movement of W. H. Auden, for instance, from socialism to Christianity over the decade 1929–1939 is another instance of the same axiological shift. One can also find the two opposites dangerously conflated in a typical 1930s poem such as C. Day Lewis's *Magnetic Mountain,* for instance in the following lines from the well-known section that begins "You that love England":

You who go out alone, in tandem or on pillion,
Down arterial roads riding in April,
Or sad beside lakes where hill-slopes are reflected
Making fires of leaves, your high hopes fallen:
Cyclists and hikers in company, day excursionists,
Refugees from cursed towns and devastated areas:
Know you seek a new world, a saviour to establish
Long-lost kinship and restore the blood's fulfillment.
. . . .
. . . We can tell you a secret, offer a tonic; only
Submit to the visiting angel, the strange new healer.
. . . .
. . . You shall be leaders when zero hour is signalled,
Wielders of power and welders of a new world.

[Skelton, 49–50]

This poem, which first appeared in the tendentious collection *New Country* in 1933, is a communist manifesto, written by a committed party member, but the rhetoric of savior and angel is thoroughly imbued with Christian iconography, as if Day Lewis could express his hopes convincingly only through figures of speech that he should have repudiated. The poem is also marked by a deeply felt sense of place that is just a step from nationalism: "You that love England, who have an ear for her music." Similarly, "the visiting angel, the strange new healer," may refer to your local CP recruiter, but it exudes disturbing connotations of the *Führer-Prinzip*: "Submit." One of the other structuring polarities of modernism is defined by the opposition between equality and hierarchy or, in more purely political terms, between democratic and authoritarian notions of government. This is a polarity that existed *within* the socialist movement itself, however, and not simply as a difference between socialism and conservative or reactionary persuasions.

We shall be returning to Joyce, but first it will be useful to undertake a reading of the life of another young man of Joyce's generation who was caught in the same ideological web. He was born in the early 1880s into a family with little money, though they managed nonetheless to send him away to religious boarding schools. A biographer described his father as one who "like his son after him nurtured a mixture of contradictory ideals" (2). His father's carelessness about money made life a struggle for the family. At school the young man was troubled by illness and was punished by the authorities. He preferred reading to playing with the other children. At one point he led a revolt against the quality of the food. He refused to go to mass and once had to be dragged to church by force. In his second school his interest in music flourished and he was asked to give a speech at a local theatre in honor of a famous composer. At the age of 17 he was known as a hermit and misanthrope, but he made regular visits to a local brothel. He received his diploma shortly after the turn of the century, at which time his biographer describes him in this way: "There was already much of the intellectual bohemian about him. He was writing poems and trying, if unsuccessfully, to get them published. He knew long passages of Dante by heart and was a voracious reader of novels and political tracts" (5).

After a brief job as a substitute teacher, borrowing money from a number of people, he went into self-imposed exile, leaving behind debts and unpaid rent. In his adopted country he drifted from one job to another. He was a socialist but he had, his biographer tells us, "little patience with sentimental reformist socialism or with democratic and parliamentary methods; instead he preached revolution to expropriate a ruling class that would never voluntarily renounce power and possessions" (7). He spent some time in Paris in 1904 but did not settle there. He worked on foreign languages and practiced translating books from both French and German. He taught school briefly but had trouble keeping order. His biographer tells us that "his mother's death at the age of forty-six caused him great grief and perhaps some feelings of guilt for having been so inattentive a son" (9). He spent hours in a university library "on a somewhat rambling and random course of reading that later stood him in good stead" (8). He set up housekeeping and started a family in a one-room apartment in the Italian part of Austria with a woman he later married, who is described as taking no interest in his writing or in politics and having "no intellectual pursuits of her own" (16). A knowledgeable observer has described his political views while in his early self-imposed exile as follows: "more the reflection of his early environment than the product of understanding and conviction; his hatred of oppression was not that impersonal hatred of a system shared by all revolutionaries; it sprang rather from his own sense of indignity and frustration, from a passion to assert his own ego" (11). He tried his hand at both journalism and fiction but had trouble finding a publisher for his fiction.

Whose early life is described in this brief sketch? It is much like that of James Augustine Aloysius Joyce, is it not, this early life of the man christened Benito Andrea Amilcare Mussolini? Joyce, of course, was named after three saints and Mussolini after three left-wing revolutionaries, but the patterns of their early lives are strikingly similar. In describing Mussolini's youth I have carefully followed Denis Mack Smith's biography (all the above page references were to this text), only I have suppressed the repeated incidents of physical violence and brutality that distinguished the personality of the young Mussolini from that of the young Joyce. Mussolini was apparently quick to rape a reluctant female or stab an antagonistic male, actions that situate him at an enormous distance from the essentially gentle and monogamous Irishman. This violence led to a number of imprisonments that also distinguish the youth of Mussolini from that of Joyce. There are other differences as well, in class background, for instance, but these very differences emphasize the strikingly similar patterns in the lives of these two young men who were born a year apart in two troubled countries.

Joyce seems to have abandoned socialism—and all political commitment—some time before war broke out in 1914, though I believe
his socialistic views were entirely serious in the days when he was
reading *Avanti!* and describing himself as a socialistic artist. Mussolini, of course, was fervent enough as a socialist to become the
editor of *Avanti!* in 1912, at which time he also tried to establish
another journal named *Utopia* in honor of St. Thomas More, whom
he admired as the first socialist. For two years at *Avanti!* Mussolini
upheld the international socialist line, but as the war approached he
became more nationalistic, to the point where he was expelled from
his editorship in November 1914 and by December had founded the
first *fascio d'azione rivoluzionaria*. In November 1906, at the height of
his interest in socialism, Joyce had expressed his admiration for
Arthur Griffith and said in a letter to his brother, "If the Irish pro-
gramme did not insist on the Irish language I suppose I could call
myself a nationalist" (*Letters*, 187). Both Joyce and Mussolini were
caught up in a similar tide running from internationalism toward
nationalism. This polarity between international and national commitment was a structuring element of the modernist dialectic for
several decades, ultimately being rewritten as a battle between socialism and fascism. The Stalinist move to "socialism in one country,"
preserving the Russian revolution by sacrificing a number of others, is
a response to the same nationalistic surge in the ideology of modern
Europe felt by Joyce and Mussolini a decade or so earlier. For Mussolini, fascism was the answer to his disillusionment with international socialism. As his Fascist Party developed after the war, gaining
more and more power, he gradually discarded the socialist elements of
his program, abandoning both his anticlericalism and his sympathy
for the proletariat. What he kept was his attitude toward parliamentary forms of government, an attitude highly visible in the *Avanti!* of
1906, for instance, which Joyce read and discussed regularly.

The view of parliamentary government that Joyce found most appropriate in the latter part of 1906 was that expressed by the syndicalist
Arturo Labriola. Joyce explained this in a letter to Stanislaus which is
worth quoting at some length:

I am following with interest the struggle between the various socialist parties here at the Congress. Labriola spoke yesterday, the paper says, with extraordinarily rapid eloquence for two hours and a half. He reminds me somewhat of Griffith. He attacked the intellectuals and the parliamentary socialists. He belongs or is leader of the sindicalists. . . . They assert that they are the true socialists because they wish the future social order to proceed equally from the overthrow of the entire present social organization and from the automatic emergence of the proletariat in trades-unions and guilds and the like. Their objection to parliamentarianism seems to me well-founded . . . Of course the sindicalists are anti-militarists but I don't see how that saves them from the conclusion of revolution in a conscriptive country like this. [*Letters*, 173–74]

We should notice a number of things in Joyce's analysis, including his lack of faith in parliamentary government (which we Americans usually refer to as democracy), a position which he also takes in other letters of this period. The evidence suggests that he accepted the socialist critique of parliaments as tools of the bourgeois oligarchy for maintaining its own power and wealth. Certainly his hatred for what he called "the stupid, dishonest, tyrannical, and cowardly burgher class" (*Letters*, 158) and "these insolent whores of the bureaucracy" (164) is well documented.

Joyce's connection of Arturo Labriola to Arthur Griffith is also interesting, but the truly devastating point of his commentary on the syndicalists is his dismissal of any possibility of obtaining power for the proletariat other than through revolution. He is quick to reject (in another part of the passage from which I have already quoted at length) the syndicalist dream of a general strike. The most damning thing he says against the syndicalists is that they have come to resemble the English socialists. They repress the necessity for revolution because they ignore the fact that "the Italian army is not directed against the Austrian army so much as against the Italian people." In the years when Joyce gave his serious attention to politics, he favored a revolution that would suppress parliamentary government, expropriate the vast wealth of the Catholic Church (*Letters*, 165–66), punish the bourgeoisie, and emancipate the proletariat (198). This became, in fact, the program of Mussolini's Fascists, until Mussolini abandoned the genuinely socialist elements of it in 1921, retaining only its antiparliamentarity.

I do not wish to suggest that Joyce was a protofascist in 1906 but to point out that he had attended carefully enough to the dialogue of the Italian socialists for some years to see the overwhelming problems facing the socialist enterprise in Italy, which boiled down to the question, How do pacifist internationalists make a national revolution in a country with a standing army? It took a world war to answer that question, and even in Russia after 1917 it finally took the authoritarian nationalism of Stalin to sustain that revolution. Joyce's turn away from politics, which took place around the time we have been examining, was no doubt determined by many things, among them the impossible contradictions he discerned in the political position he found most congenial. But there is more to the story of Joyce's socialism than this, and we must examine certain features of it more thoroughly to discover what he learned during his political years.

For the space of about a year, in 1906 and 1907, when he was finishing *Dubliners* and planning *A Portrait* and his "story" *Ulysses*, Joyce thought of himself—frequently and earnestly—as a socialist. After that period he certainly took less interest in politics, but he neither repudiated his earlier views nor adopted any of the political alternatives that were so visible and insistent around him. We are generally less aware than we should be of Joyce's socialism, mainly because Richard Ellmann, who was in most respects an exemplary steward of the Joycean oeuvre, adopted a view of Joyce that did not admit of a serious commitment of this sort, at one point in the biography observing, "At heart Joyce can scarcely have been a Nietzschean any more than he was a socialist" (147), and at another arguing that any interest Joyce took in socialism was motivated by a petty hope for personal gain, believing that "the triumph of socialism might make for some sort of state subsidy of artists like himself" (204).

It is a wise biographer who knows the heart of his subject, but Ellmann is not seeing into a heart, of course; he is reading and writing the life of a literary artist as a young man. His young man frequently returned to the theme of socialism in letters to his brother. Ellmann's way of acknowledging this is to say that Joyce "labored to make socialism an integral part of his personality," the implication clearly being that such labor was in vain; but producing an integrated personality is more the biographer's problem than his subject's. Consider, for a moment, the passage Ellmann introduced into the biography from the letters as an example of Joyce's vain labor:

It is a mistake for you to imagine that my political opinions are those of a universal lover: but they are those of a socialist artist. I cannot tell you how strange I feel sometimes in my attempt to lead a more civilized life than my contemporaries. But why should I have brought Nora to a priest or a lawyer to make her swear away her life to me? And why should I superimpose on my child the very troublesome burden of belief which my father and mother superimposed on me? Some people would answer that while professing to be a socialist I am trying to make money: but this is not quite true at least as they mean it. [Ellmann, 205]

The passage goes on for some distance. What it reveals, among other things, is that for Joyce his rejections of church and state in his own life—as represented by rejection of formal marriage and baptism or religious instruction for children—are aspects of what he calls his socialism. Ellmann's comment on all this is a laconic put-down: "socialism has rarely been defended so tortuously" (205). Unfortunately, socialism has rarely been defended in any other way than tortuously, as a little reading in Marx, Adorno, or Lukács would quickly demonstrate—and there are overwhelming reasons why this has been so. One cannot argue for a new way of thinking within an old way of thinking except with the kind of self-conscious complexity that is all too easily dismissed as "tortuous." My purpose here, however, is not to defend socialistic discourse but to explore the ways in which socialism and other ideological currents merged and diverged during the period that we call modernist. In particular I am interested in the ways in which European culture at this time functioned as a text, shaping the minds of individuals who later helped to change the literary and political map of Europe.

One of the ways in which this culture functioned textually was through actual printed texts that passed along cultural presupposi-

tions to the next generation. Ferrero's *L'Europa giovane* was such a
book. As Joyce recounts in letters his reading of this book we can see it
influencing him and we can also see him reading it in his own way,
taking from it ideas, feelings, and even phrases that he will incorporate
into his own textual apparatus. Ferrero was a classical liberal human-
ist, a true child of the Enlightenment. It is also true that he was
infected by nineteenth-century racism to some extent. His explana-
tions of behavior according to racial characteristics appear ludicrous
now, but there is much in *L'Europa giovane* that is still interesting.
Joyce's "tortuous" defense of his socialism no doubt owes something
to passages like this one:

A man can become a socialist through class interest; that is, because he sees
in the socialist party the best defense of his own interest. But a man can
also become a socialist against the interest of his class, for moral reasons,
because the numerous defects and the many vices of modern society have
disgusted him; and that is the case of many bourgeois socialists,
independent professionals, scientists, rich people, who in many countries
of Europe, and especially in Italy, participate in one way or another in the
socialist movement. [361, my translation]

That is not so bad for 1897. Ferrero was friendly to socialism and
accepted much of Marx's criticism of bourgeois society as justified,
but he thought that when it came to the crucial matter of the future,
Marx had substituted Semitic religiosity for the science he claimed to
profess. Joyce told Stanislaus in a letter of November 1906 that he had
just finished reading Ferrero's *L'Europa giovane*. His reports on what
he had read show him as a centripetal or exorbitant reader, conflating,
rearranging, and altering emphases as he adapted Ferrero's textuality
to his own. He was especially interested in Ferrero's observations on
Jews, Jewishness, and anti-Semitism. Here are excerpts from a passage that must have greatly interested the young Irishman:

The great men of the Hebrews have almost all had a transcendent
consciousness of their own missions . . . ; they have all felt themselves,
more or less lucidly, to be Messiahs. The old popular legend has become a
living sentiment, a reality, in the consciousness of the great representatives
of the race. Every great Hebraic man is persuaded, even if he does not say

so, of having a mandate to inaugurate a new era for the world; to make, in the abyss of darkness in which humanity lives, the opening through which will enter for the first time, and forever, the light of truth. Of course this consciousness may be more or less clear, take one form or another, have a greater or lesser amplitude according to times and individuals, but it is there in all of them; it is in Jesus come to announce the heavenly kingdom; it is in Marx come to announce the proletarian revolution; it is in Lombroso, come to deliver the true scales of justice, after so many ages in which men through ignorance and malice have adopted the false. [Ferrero, 366, my translation]

This passage obviously made an impact on Joyce, providing much of what he reported to his brother in his letters about Ferrero, but it also provided something else: a verbal formula that came in handy when Joyce sought a ringing phrase for the conclusion of his first novel. Consider it again, this time in Italian: "La vecchia leggenda del popolo è diventata sentimento vivo e realta nella coscienza . . . della razza." Not Marx and Mary but Marx and Jesus are conflated here by Ferrero as embodying a legend that had become a reality in the consciousness of their race. The oddity of the Joycean version of this phrase—"to forge in the smithy of my soul the uncreated conscience of my race"— can be traced to its too literal echo of the Italian ("conscience" for "consciousness" because of "coscienza") and also to Joyce's rewriting of the phrase to suit the Irish, who, in his view, lacked precisely that Jewish racial conscience and, therefore, needed an artist to provide for them what the biblical texts had provided for the Jews. An artist who was also a bit of a messiah might be exactly the right thing to turn the Irish from what he once called a "rabblement" into a race.

Ferrero contributed something important to the creation of both Stephen Dedalus and Leopold Bloom (as Dominic Manganiello noted in his important book *Joyce's Politics*) and to the way in which Joyce pictured his own literary enterprise during the writing of *Dubliners* and *A Portrait*. In a letter to Grant Richards, Joyce once characterized *Dubliners* as written "for the most part in a style of scrupulous meanness" (*Letters*, 133–34). Stanislaus Joyce claimed (in *My Brother's Keeper*, 204) that this phrase was a rewriting of words he had used in a letter to his brother three years earlier, in which he suggested that meanness, if "studious" or careful, could be a virtue in a writer. This may be so, but the immediate stimulus for this well-known phrase must have been a passage in Ferrero. In the famous letter defending his stories "Counterparts" and "Two Gallants," Joyce mentioned Ferrero explicitly, shortly before saying that his intention was to "write a chapter in the moral history" of his country, "in a style of scrupulous meanness." Both the intent to create a conscience for his countrymen and the notion of an appropriate style can be traced with considerable certainty to Ferrero, who described the treatment of sensual love in French novels in the following words: "Che cosa si trova in Balzac, in Zola, in Flaubert, in De Goncourt? Descrizione dell'amore sensuale, fatte bene o fatte male, fatte con scrupulosa esatezza di analista" (175). By translating this scrupulous exactitude of the analyst into "scupulous meanness" Joyce connected himself to the realistic/naturalistic tradition of the writers named by Ferrero, and he made the phrase his own by lowering the tone of "esatezza" to suit the sordid paralysis he felt was centered in Dublin. Watching Joyce read and rewrite Ferrero helps us to understand the microprocesses by which culture shapes a powerful mind and is shaped by it.

Though the Joyce we know from his later years had become militantly antipolitical (deploring, for instance, the fact that at a PEN meeting in Paris in 1937, the exiled Guglielmo Ferrero insisted on lecturing passionately against the burning of books by the fascists—this, in what I believe was the only meeting between the two men), the earlier Joyce was a very different person. Certainly, we can no longer ignore the fact that the writer of *Dubliners* and other early works felt himself to be engaged in bringing to consciousness the social problems that beset his nation, or, in his own—and Ferrero's—language, creating a conscience for his race. We know enough about him at this point to attempt a summary of his early literary and political attitudes. He was antibourgeois, anticlerical, antiparliamentary, antimilitarist, antibureaucratic, an Irish nationalist (except for language), and definitely not an anti-Semite, though intensely interested in Jews. In literature he admired Ibsen, Hauptmann, Tolstoy, and Maupassant. What he did not like is well expressed in his comments on George Gissing in a letter of November 1906:

I have read Gissing's *Demos: A Story of English Socialism*. Why are English novels so terribly boring? I think G has little merit. The socialist in this is first a worker and then inherits a fortune, jilts his first girl, marries a lydy, becomes a big employer and takes to drink. You know the kind of story. There is a clergyman in it with searching eyes and a deep voice who makes all the socialists wince under his firm gaze. [*Letters*, 186]

In this critique, Joyce's socialism and anticlericalism are inextricably bound up with his sense of realities and his aesthetic judgment. He is judging by a standard in which realism and aestheticism are allied, rather than antagonistic, which is very significant, because it shows him resisting one of the binarisms that had characterized the cultural practice out of which literary modernism emerged and against which it positioned itself. At the end of the nineteenth century, European fiction was shaped by the fragmentation of what had been a unified realism—often embodied in the omniscience of a narrative voice—into the opposed extremes of aestheticism and naturalism: as in Wilde and Gissing, for instance. In the early moments of literary modernism, as I am reading (or writing) them, we find the most perceptive and talented writers trying to reunite these divided impulses (think of *The Waste Land* or the work of Picasso's Blue Period, for instance). Later on, in my version of this story, the attempt to reunite naturalism and aestheticism is abandoned (as in the later work of Joyce and Picasso). In 1906, however, Joyce was trying to hold things together, seeking a way of extending realism, without it fragmenting into aesthetic and naturalistic poles. Certainly the stories of *Dubliners* can usefully be seen in exactly that light. It will be helpful in appreciating Joyce's position to look carefully at his thoughts on a writer whom most critics would see as tending toward the naturalistic pole to a greater extent than Tolstoy, Maupassant, or Ibsen—all of whom he admired—may be said to do. I refer to Gerhart Hauptmann, whose *Rosa Bernd* Joyce acquired, though he could scarcely afford it, at a time in the summer of 1906 when he was also taking lessons in order to read Ibsen more easily in the original. Joyce had admired Hauptmann for some years, but his appraisal of this playwright's work was well this side of idolatry:

I finished Hauptmann's *Rosa Bernd* on Sunday. I wonder if he acts well. His plays, when read, leave an unsatisfying impression on the reader. Yet he must have the sense of the stage well developed in him by now. He never, in his later plays at least, tries for a curtain so that the ends of his acts seem ruptures of a scene. His characters appear to be more highly vivified by their creator than Ibsen's but they are also less under control. He has a difficulty in subordinating them to the action of his drama. He deals with life quite differently, more frankly at certain points . . . but also so broadly that my personal conscience is seldom touched. His way of treating such types as Arnold Kramer and Rosa Bernd is, however, altogether to my taste. His temperament has a little of Rimbaud in it. Like him, too, I suppose somebody else will be his future. But, after all, he has written two or three masterpieces—"a little immortal thing" like *The Weavers*, for example. I have found nothing of the charlatan in him yet. [*Letters*, 173]

Joyce's praise of Hauptmann's vividness of characterization, his frankness, and his freedom from charlatanry is balanced by a dissatisfaction that is partly aesthetic (a disparity between characters and actions) and partly ethical: he deals with life "so broadly that my personal conscience is not touched." Joyce's way of reading Hauptmann—made only partly explicit here—is to situate him against Ibsen, whose control and balance bring him near the top of Joyce's aesthetic scale. The young Joyce's reactions to Gissing and Hauptmann can help us to locate his own position with respect to naturalism. He rejects the sentimentalized naturalism of Gissing and prefers the harsher, franker naturalism of Hauptmann. But he is troubled by two features of Hauptmann's work, a certain lack of aesthetic "control" (which Ibsen so obviously had) and a crudity or broadness that left Joyce's "personal conscience" untouched—a criticism similar to Ferrero's critique of the French novelists. The need to reconcile the naturalistic presentation of life with an aesthetic control that would affect the personal conscience emerges from these critiques as the central problem for Joyce as a writer. It is the paradigmatic problem for the modernist writer of plays or stories, a problem that other modernists, such as Hemingway and Lawrence, would also have to solve.

This problem became central in the work of another young man of Joyce's generation, whose experience will serve to complete this attempt at a reading of modernist ideology. He was born in the 1880s in a city on the edge of Europe. Though raised in a bourgeois family he rebelled against bourgeois manners and values. He was a bright student in school: outwardly conforming but inwardly rebellious. One of the earliest works to impress him was the Lambs' *Tales from Shakespeare* (which also meant much to Joyce as a child). At a later age he discovered "Baudelaire, Verlaine, Swinburne, Zola, Ibsen, and Tolstoy as leaders and guides (147). As he matured, he continued to admire the radicalism of Scandinavian and Russian literature. Years later he recalled his relationship with his family in this way:

I was completely estranged from my family, or at least from a part of it. I did not have any relationship with the family at all. . . . My mother was a shrewd woman who soon saw what was happening. She fell seriously ill and died of cancer of the breast. Under pressure from other members of the family, I wrote her a letter. When she received it she said, "I must be very ill for [my son] to write me a letter." [35]

Rejecting marriage as a bourgeois convention he went into self-imposed exile. Looking back on his twenty-third year he wrote, "In my case . . , absolute independence in order to produce, and for that reason silent rejection" (151). This was his version of the Joycean "silence, exile, and cunning," which aesthetically inclined young men of this generation adopted as a protective posture. He came to admire the work of a poet who expressed his own values, seeing in this poet in 1906, as he later recalled, "a revolutionary who regarded the revolution as indispensable for his own self-realization" (39) just as Joyce and Mussolini apparently did. He had ambitions to write a treatise on aesthetics and to be a dramatist. "I started," he tells us, "to write plays in the manner of Hauptmann and Ibsen" and he translated *The Wild Duck* into his native language (*Record of a Life*, 31, 34—previous citations are also to this work). Writing about Hauptmann some time after his youthful enthusiasm, he praised in particular the dramatist's "great and beautiful honesty" (*Reviews and Articles*, l27–28). Living in Italy in his twenty-sixth year, he began a major work on aesthetic theory but set it aside the following year. When he was about twenty-five, he discovered French syndicalism, which, he says, "at that time I regarded as the only oppositional socialist movement that could be taken seriously" (*Record of a Life*, 41). He condemned conditions in his own country, which he seriously hoped to change through his own work, but, as he has said, "this did not mean that I was prepared to accept English Parliamentarianism as an alternative ideal."

The young man I have been describing, as you have no doubt realized, is Georg Lukács, the Hungarian Jew who became Europe's leading Marxist literary critic and theoretician. Considering the fact that he came to be a major opponent of the kind of modernism he felt to be manifested in Joyce's work, it is useful to see how much the two writers shared in the cultural matrix from which modernism emerged. But at the point where Joyce turned from politics to art, Lukács turned in the opposite direction. At the end of his life an interviewer asked him about this shift of interest:

Int: You said you gave up aesthetics because you had begun to be interested in ethical problems. What works resulted from this interest?

G. L.: At that time it did not result in any written works. My interest in ethics led me to the revolution. [*Record of a Life*, 53]

Both of these young men reached a similar point of decision and made their choices, living the lives that followed from them. They had also made other choices, Joyce abandoning criticism as Lukács abandoned drama, but these were more personal, matters of talent, primarily. Perhaps the ideological choices stem as much from personality as anything else, but there is a lot we do not know about these things. In the case of Joyce, for instance, what may have been a crucial year of intellectual decision, 1908, is simply a blank page on the biographical record. For the first eleven months of that year, we have five lines of correspondence and precious little else. We know a lot about what Joyce was in 1906 and what he later became. About the transition itself, we are ignorant.

We know, however, that Georg Lukács became the most articulate critical opponent of modernism in literature (with the possible exception of Wyndham Lewis). Lukács's critique of modernism has a philosophical basis that allows him to set modernism against realism, even to see modernism as a perverse negation of realism. For Lukács, realism is based on the view of man as a *zoon politikon*, a political animal. Modernism, on the other hand, is based on a view of human existence as, in Heidegger's expression, a *Geworfenheit ins Dasein*, a "thrownness into Being." Realism, says Lukács, depends upon perspective and norms of human behavior, whereas modernism destroys perspective and glorifies the abnormal. Realism assumes the objectivity of time and modernism assumes time's subjectivity. For Lukács, Joyce acquired the proportions of the archmodernist, whose works displayed an exaggerated concern with form, style, and technique in general, along with an excessive attention to sense data, combined with a comparative neglect of ideas and emotions.

Lukács's unfavorable comparison of Joyce to Thomas Mann, however, has affinities with Joyce's comparison of Hauptmann to Ibsen. It should also be noted that Lukács does not trivialize Joyce's enterprise He is perfectly ready to call *Ulysses* a masterpiece, as he does in the following passage:

A gifted writer, however extreme his theoretical modernism, will in practice have to compromise with the demands of historicity and of social environment. Joyce uses Dublin, Kafka and Musil the Hapsburg Monarchy, as the locus of their masterpieces. But the locus they lovingly depict is little more than a backcloth, it is not basic to their artistic intention. [*Realism*, 21]

Lukács particularly criticized Joyce's use of the stream of consciousness, in which, as he argued, "the perpetually oscillating patterns of sense and memory data, their powerfully charged— but aimless and directionless—fields of force, give rise to an epic structure which is static, reflecting a belief in the basically static character of events" (*Realism*, 18). This is by no means a trivial or inaccurate description of Joyce's practice, though I think the Joycean stream of consciousness is more directed and purposeful that Lukács gives it credit for being. Lukács is surely right, however, when he borrows Walter Benjamin's description of Romantic and Baroque art to characterize the allegorical tendencies of modernism: "Every person, every object, every relationship can stand for something else" (*Realism*, 42). It is surely this, and the Joycean sense that history is an endless repetition of such transformations, that makes Joyce a fearful object to Lukács, whose faith in progressive possibilities leads him to abhor what he called the "religious atheism" that animated Joyce's modernism.

For all their differences, however, they were products of very similar cultural interests and pressures. To emphasize that, I shall close this comparative reading of the two writers by presenting some excerpts from one of the last things Lukács wrote, his *Gelebtes Denken* or preliminary notes for an autobiography that he did not live to finish. To my ears they connect him across time, across politics, across experiences, across Europe, with the writer who most symbolized for him the mistaken ways of modernist prose. Listen. Read.

Objectivity: the correct historicity. Memory: tendency to relocate in time. Check against the facts. Youth. . . .

No poet. Only a philosopher. Abstractions. Memory, too, organized to that end. Danger: premature generalization of spontaneous experience. But poets: able to recall concrete feelings. . . . That already means at the right place at the right time. Especially: childhood. . . .

Live here: over 80—subjective interest in reality maintained—at a time when the contact with early youth often lost. Long and even now, an undeniably industrious life—my right to attempt to justify this posture. [*Record of a Life*, 143–44]

Thus an old Hungarian Jew, back from exile, planning to justify his life, lapses into a prose somewhere between an outline and a stream of consciousness. He wants to fight the tendency of memory to relocate in subjective time, he seeks the objective, the facts, but he also says, wistfully, "No poet, only a philosopher. Abstractions." He fought to the end his own culturally induced inclination toward modernism and the power of his modernized subjectivity, which had been formed in the same European crucible as those he criticized.

This has been a long excursion into the lives of the modernists, but some density was required to make such a seemingly absurd project plausible at all. But whether I have done it well or ill is not so important as the possibility of its being done. I hope I have done it at least well enough to induce others to do it better and to demonstrate that it makes sense to read lives as texts and to think of reading as a matter of making connections between one text and others. This is how reading functions as a centrifugal and intertextual activity. In this chapter as a whole I have tried to present reading as a constructive activity in which, in Barthes's words, we rewrite "the text of the work within the text of our lives." We shall return to the question of how books and lives are related at the end of chapter 3, but now it is time to approach the process of reading from the other point of view—as a centripetal activity, in which we seek to eliminate irrelevancies and close the circle of meaning as tightly as we can. Under the heading of "protocols," we will consider the problem of devising some method that would guarantee the validity of readings.

Two

Interpretation: The Question of Protocols

Reading is transformational. . . . But this transformation cannot be executed however one wishes. It requires protocols of reading. Why not say it bluntly: I have not yet found any that satisfy me.

Jacques Derrida

Interpretation is a problem because human beings live in time. The person who reads a text is never the person who wrote it—even if they are the "same" person. To the extent that our reading is a rewriting of the text, along the lines developed in chapter 1, this is not a problem. The reader as writer proceeds by constructing metaphors, metonymies, and causalities: developing his or her own metatext. But reading is also—and always—an attempt to grasp meanings that are not ours, meanings that are interesting precisely because they come from outside us. In reading we find ourselves, to be sure, but only through the language of the Other, whose existence we must respect for reasons that I shall try briefly to explain. We must respect the Other in the text because, as human beings, we have a dimension that is irreducibly social. We have been constructed as human subjects by interacting with other people, learning their language and their ways of behaving. Having come to consciousness in this way, we have an

absolute need for communication. As human subjects we must exchange meanings with others whom we recognize as subjects like
ourselves, whose desire to communicate we need to respect, in order
to confirm our own right to be treated as subjects rather than objects.
In every act of reading the irreducible otherness of writer and reader is
balanced and opposed by this need for recognition and understanding
between the two parties. As readers we cannot ignore the intentions
of writers without an act of textual violence that threatens our own
existence as textual beings. But neither can we ever close the commu-
nicative gap completely—and in many cases we must acknowledge
that the gap is very wide indeed.

We need protocols of reading for the same reason that we need
other codes and customs—because we desire a framework in which to
negotiate our differences. These are not issues confined to literature
and the arts. All our cherished texts—political, religious, and artistic—are locked in languages or styles of thought and representation
that become further removed from our own with every passing year.
For a specific reminder of these problems we can return to the frontis-
piece of this book, which we considered at the beginning of chapter 1.
This painting probably has an origin in the work of Georges de La
Tour around 1645–50. It is itself an interpretation of earlier texts, a
gloss on the life of the Virgin (if we can trust the title). La Tour is
separated from biblical times by an enormous gap, made wider by the
lack in his immediate culture of a historical (or historistic) consciousness. His way of reading or seeing the ancient past involves
assimilating it to his own time. This act presupposes a certain innocence or naivety about historical matters that is beyond our imaginative reach. Even to call it "innocence or naivety" adds to this past just
the historical awareness that we find lacking in it. We cannot even
name it without doing violence to it. To read La Tour's painting we
must somehow respect his situation and whatever intentions we may
attribute to him, but we cannot and should not suppress our own
knowledge about the matters to which he has addressed himself in the
painting. All this, of course, is complicated by the fact that we are not
sure whether this work was done in his workshop, by his son or
someone else, whether it is based on a lost original, who gave it the

title it bears, and so on. The status of the text is in question. The author is in question. The title is in question. Nevertheless, we read it as a work of Georges de La Tour called *The Education of the Virgin* because there is reasonable evidence that supports our doing so, and we read it as a contribution to our discussion of protocols of reading because it helps to illuminate an important dimension of that problem.

What we cannot do, of course, is ask La Tour what book his Virgin is reading—and this is not just because he has been dead for three hundred years and more but because to pose the question from our perspective would shatter the entire world in which La Tour lived. We are faced with irreducible, irremediable otherness here: the otherness of reading writ large. He was faced with the same problem himself, of course, but he could not be aware of it as acutely as we are. It is characteristic of our own time that we are aware of this problem almost to the point of paralysis. This has become the age of interpretation because we see the need for interpretation everywhere. Indeed, we have come to believe that interpretation can triumph over almost any brute event or fact. It is not what has happened that counts but what "spin" the event can be given in media textuality, and we have coined the expression "spin doctor" for those whose job it is to manipulate the interpretation of public events. The problem is that we are now perhaps excessively aware of the gap between any event and its entry into textuality. We know that we have no more direct access to a pretextualized event than we do to the author of a written text, and we suffer from that knowledge. In our world, nothing stands still.

One reaction to this state of affairs can be called "fundamentalist," without implying any specific religious connection. Textual fundamentalism is the belief that texts always say just what they mean, so that any honest or decent person ought to be able to understand this perfectly clear meaning without making any fuss about it. The problem with this position is that it requires an infallible author, a perfect language, and a timeless context in order to work. If we wish to think of any current English-language Bible as conveying God's intentions in a fundamental way, for instance, we have to assume not only that the actual writers of the original text were thoroughly inspired by a perfect Being, but also that the Hebrew language had been perfected as the vehicle for this inspired discourse, that the English translators were as inspired as the original transcribers of God's Word, that the English language had been perfected as the vehicle for the Hebrew, and that modern revisions of that text have brought it into alignment with what we must admit is a historically changing context. But if we admit that meaning is tied to context and that contexts change throughout history, then we must admit—at the very least—that at certain times, between revisions, the text has been in need of interpretation. With respect to the New Testament, of course, we have to assume that events that were enacted in Aramaic and other languages of the region where Jesus lived could be reported in Greek without any distortion of their historical truth, and translated into English and revised for modern readers without any distortion.

The fundamentalist view of interpretation requires two things: that meaning be fixed eternally, outside of time, and that texts in time-bound languages convey that meaning so directly that it can be discerned without interpretation. Fundamentalist attempts to fix the meaning of texts all—without exception—can be shown to require some timeless zone in which true meanings are said to reside. "A text means what its author intends it to mean" is a refrain we still hear today (from fundamentalist theoreticians such as Steven Knapp and Walter Benn Michaels, for instance, in *Against Theory*), but the use of the perpetual present tense in these formulations betrays the nostalgia for eternity that governs all such enterprises. And even if we allow that eternity has a place in biblical interpretation, we cannot treat secular texts under the aspect of eternity. Human authors exist in time. Their intentions change—even during the writing of a single text. And often those intentions are vague or incomplete to begin with. The modern discipline of hermeneutics is founded upon the awareness of such problems. It was Dilthey, not Freud, who said in a lecture delivered almost a century ago that "the final goal of hermeneutic procedure is to understand the author better than he understood himself; a statement which is the necessary conclusion of the doctrine of unconscious creation" (259–60). Most students of interpretation today accept some version of this view and assume that in any text the reader

will find traces of both conscious intention and unconscious intention, making any notion of a single, unified intention impossible.
Most of us assume also that human subjectivity is a vehicle for all sorts
of cultural meanings that have already shaped any individual human
consciousness. Our intentions are neither simple nor entirely our
own. Therefore we cannot express exactly what we desire to express so
that others will understand us perfectly. Let us listen to Paul Valéry on
this question:

Quant à l'interprétation de la *lettre*, je me suis déja expliqué ailleurs sur ce
point; mais on n'y insistera jamais assez. *Il n'y a pas de vrai sens d'un texte.*
Pas d'autorité de l'auteur. Quoi qu'il ait *voulu dire*, il a écrit ce qu'il a écrit.
Une fois publié, un texte est comme un appareil dont chacun peut se servir
à sa guise et selon ses moyens: il n'est pas sûr que le constructeur en use
mieux qu'un autre. Du reste, s'il sait bien ce qu'il voulait fait, cette
connaissance trouble toujours en lui la perception de ce qu'il a fait.

As for *literal* interpretation, I have already made myself clear elsewhere on
this point; but it can never be too much insisted upon: *there is no true
meaning to a text*—no author's authority. Whatever he may have *wanted to
say*, he has written what he has written. Once published, a text is like an
apparatus that anyone may use as he will and according to his ability: it is
not certain that the one who constructed it can use it better than another.
Besides, if he knows well what he meant to do, this knowledge always
disturbs his perception of what he has done. [411, my translation; emphasis
in original]

Taking intention as something that exists before the construction of a
text, Valéry suggests that no text can ever realize such intentions. This
is so partly (as his writings make clear in many places) because the
conventional nature of language makes it a clumsy tool for the expression of delicate and fleeting thoughts and feelings. Under these
conditions, a poet does the best he or she can and then abandons the
work with the intention that motivated it still somewhat unfulfilled.
The reader does the rest, producing a textual interpretation that is the
product of two consciousnesses, finding meanings that perhaps neither could be said to have "intended" before they were found but that
both would accept as appropriate.

Lest it be thought that Valéry presents some peculiarly symbolist view that is out of the main line of interpretive theory, we should note that his position is not so far as one might expect from the view developed by Dilthey in his biography of Schleiermacher. Compare him to Valéry:

> The universal which seems to permeate events and characters of true poetry need not be present in the form of a previous, rational insight. What the reader abstracts from the interweaving of characters and destinies is his own, subjectively formulated, idea which he derived from the enjoyment of the poetry, though it is not inherent in the poem itself. This explains the infinite variety of a poetic work which allows its content to be expressed in quite different conceptual interpretations but exhausted by none. We confront the poet's creations like the world itself, which also defies any final interpretation through concepts. [Dilthey, 34]

This formulation, especially in its closing words about the uninterpretable world, brings Dilthey surprisingly close to such contemporary theoreticians of interpretation as Frank Kermode, who also compares the world and the book, insisting that they are equally "unfollowable": "World and book, it may be, are hopelessly plural, endlessly disappointing; we stand alone before them, aware of their arbitrariness and impenetrability, knowing that they may be narratives only because of our impudent intervention, and susceptible of interpretation only by our hermeneutic tricks" (145). Kermode, of course, who assumes that his position is a purely contemporary one, believes of Dilthey that "he was not considering the possibility that a work of art is a kind of 'world' in which other impression-points than the one he associates with the mental constitution of the artist might be taken as the starting-point of interpretive articulations" (147 *n*). But Dilthey, at least on occasion, saw the question of interpretation in a manner very similar to that of Kermode himself, even to the point of asserting that the world and the text offer the same problems for interpretation.

There have been theories and methods of interpretation as long as there have been texts that seemed to require it— for millennia, that is—but the modern discipline of hermeneutics arose in the nineteenth century as a way of saving "truth" after the skepticism of the Enlightenment had made fundamentalism an untenable position. And with it arose a more extreme skepticism that rejected the possibilities of interpretive truth along with those of fundamental truth. For our purposes it is convenient to think of this skepticism as embodied in the person of Friedrich Nietzsche and in the attitude that he called (with a good deal of ambivalence) "nihilism." For a hundred years and more, hermeneutics and nihilism have been in active opposition at the center of our cultural dialectic. At the present time we can find both of these opposed attitudes or impulses at work in much of our best writing on interpretive questions. Both impulses are detectable in the text from Jacques Derrida (used as an epigraph for this chapter) that has given this book its title, for instance, and it is their presence together in such texts that leads me to pose the question of whether we may be moving toward some sort of reconciliation or sublation of the two. My main consideration in this chapter will be whether such a practice—let us call it a nihilistic hermeneutics—can be developed and sustained. I believe that many of our most interesting textual interpreters and critics are operating in or near this mode already, because this is where the struggle of hermeneutics with nihilism has led us. If Frank Kermode, for instance, is practicing a nihilistic hermeneutics—and I think it fair to say that he is—it is not because he has made a radical break with the tradition of Dilthey but because he is further along the same road.

We should be aware that the contemporary attempt to arrive at a nihilistic hermeneutics is being conducted in a cultural situation in which many alternative views are being proposed, one of which we can call "vulgar nihilism." This is the view that, since there is no Truth there is no error either, and all beliefs are equal. It is not my purpose here to contend with vulgar nihilism, or with fundamentalism, or even with the various versions of solipsism and cultural relativism that abound today (though I would recommend Hilary Putnam's brief but devastating critique of cultural relativism in *Realism and Reason*, 235–36, to those who are interested). I intend, rather, to investigate the alternative to vulgar nihilism that I find in the writing of Jacques Derrida. In doing so, I shall not be expounding what I take to be

Derrida's position so much as exploring both the possibilities and the problems in that position as he has articulated it. In short, I shall be reading, interpreting, and criticizing some of the texts that have appeared under his name. It should be clear throughout, however, even where I am most critical, that I admire this work. Indeed, I have chosen to discuss it here precisely because I find the problems of interpretation so powerfully articulated in Derrida's writing. To clarify these problems, I shall sometimes situate his positions against those of a very different thinker, Stanley Rosen. Rosen's position on the issues of interpretation was developed richly in a series of books on Plato, Hegel, and nihilism itself before being deployed somewhat more polemically in his recent study *Hermeneutics as Politics*, in which he meets the contemporary enemy head on.

Like Steven Knapp and Walter Benn Michaels, Rosen takes a position "against" contemporary theory, but not from the fundamentalist direction. Rosen's view owes much to Plato, but his Plato was no fundamentalist. His argument against contemporary theory is based upon the logically powerful position that a nihilistic hermeneutics is impossible because the concepts of nihilism and hermeneutics cannot be reconciled. If *hermeneutics* refers to the search for truth or grounded meaning in texts (or the method or principles governing that search) and *nihilistic* refers to the view that truth (or grounded meaning) can never be attained, then nihilistic hermeneutics is indeed the paradoxical name of an impossible practice. My own view is that we need some such name —paradoxical or not—while we grope toward some new protocols of reading. In addition to this, I claim that the best way to deal with our situation is not to avoid but to work through the problems—both conscious and unconscious—presented by Derridean deconstruction. Rosen presents a useful challenge to my position because he argues vigorously that "a theory of interpretation is impossible upon the premises of contemporary theoreticians of interpretation" (174). By "contemporary theoreticians," in this instance, he means such writers as Richard Rorty, whom he calls a "cheerful nihilist" (183), and Jacques Derrida, whom he positions with other French postmodernists as deriving from "Heidegger's interpretation of Anaximander, with the crucial difference that *Sein* is replaced by

Nichts" (179). That is, Rosen sees Derrida and the other postmodernists, instead of saying with Heidegger that beings are the false disguises of Being, as saying that beings are the creatures of an active Nothing called *différance*. In Rosen's view, this leaves Derrida and those who share his position with no ground for a viable theory of interpretation. In a world without truth all interpretations would be equal.

With respect to vulgar nihilism, I am prepared to accept Rosen's position—but not with respect to the theory and practice of interpretation developed by Derrida. My claim will be that Derrida is a nihilist with a difference—and that there is a type of nihilism that can indeed sustain a hermeneutic. The development of this position will require some serious probing into Derrida's theory and practice of reading, including a critique of those aspects of his theories of language and interpretation that I believe to be inadequate. We can begin this inquiry with a look at his critique of Anglo-American speech act theory, of which he has said, "I am convinced that speech act theory is fundamentally and in its most fecund, most rigorous, and most interesting aspect (need I recall that it interests me considerably?) a theory of right or law, of convention, of political ethics or of politics as ethics" (*Limited Inc*, 97).

The interest that speech act theory holds for Derrida assuredly lies in its difference from his own thought. By positioning speech together with law and ethics he reaffirms, axiologically, his own position, and the position of reading as he defines it, as that of the outlaw, as what is outside or against the law. That is, of course, a centrifugal theory, which privileges the margin, the circumference at the expense of the center. The powerful appeal that Derridean thought has had for American literary critics has its emotional roots in a cultural reflex of sympathy for the outlaw, for those marginalized by culture. For American students of language and literature, the Derridean theory of reading has seemed to offer a new freedom, an exhilarating escape from stifling rules and responsibilities. This would have meant little, I believe, had not Derrida's own practice of reading—even through the medium of translation into English—exhibited concretely the possibilities of a rigorous playfulness in critical prose.

With those who admire Derrida's interpretive and critical writing I have no quarrel. I admire it myself. I also think that he has much to teach us—and has taught us much—about interpretive theory. Still, if we are to get the most from his work, we shall have to do a better job of sorting out the useful from the misleading or inadequate than we have previously done. In particular, in the following pages I shall try to show that his theory of language itself has certain serious weaknesses, and, further, that his practice as a reader diverges significantly from what many people have taken to be his theory of reading. We can begin this critique by looking into the discussions resulting from Derrida's incursion into speech act theory. My major texts will be the essay which precipitated his controversy with John Searle—"Signature Event Context"—and his response to Searle's reply, "Limited Inc a b c . . . ," both of which have been reprinted in *Limited Inc,* together with an important Afterword.

"Signature Event Context" (which I henceforth, following Derrida himself, refer to as *Sec*) offers a critique of previous theories of communication, a critique that seems to open the way toward a new and freer notion of reading. Derrida's argument in *Sec* can be summarized in the following way:

> *A written text can survive the absence of its author, the absence of its addressee, the absence of its object, the absence of its context, the absence of its code—and still be read.*

The argument also includes the stipulation that, as argued more fully elsewhere but briefly here also, what is true of writing is also true of all other forms of communication: that they are all marked, fundamentally, by the *différance* that constitutes arche-writing and is so palpable in actual written texts.

My summary is, I hope, at least tolerably fair and accurate. It is impossible to hope for more, since, as Richard Rorty admiringly remarks, Derrida "is so skillful at fishing both sides of every stream"; see Rorty's response to Henry Staten (464). I believe that this summary of *Sec*'s argument also describes, in however compressed a form, what many American teachers and critics think they have learned from Derrida: namely, that reading can be freed from responsibility to anything prior to the act of reading and, specifically, from those things named in the summary. As Derrida puts it himself: "writing is read; it is not the site, 'in the last instance,' of a hermeneutic deciphering, the decoding of a meaning or truth" (*Limited Inc*, 21).

The "last instance" here is perhaps an escape clause, meaning that in everything but the last instance (which is unattainable) hermeneutic deciphering and decoding will be in force. But it is precisely that escape clause which—aided and abetted by Derrida himself—seems to have escaped most of Derrida's American appreciators. The argument of *Sec* as I have summarized it puts tremendous pressure on the notion of reading, a pressure that increases with each stripping away of another one of the features included in most models of communication. We can begin, then, by trying to imagine what free reading—that is, reading in the absence of all the named elements of communication—would be like. Imagine, as a thought experiment, the discovery of marks—in some cave, perhaps—that have every appearance of writing but cannot be related to any known language. We could probably make sense of them. That is, we could impose meaning on them. We could invent everything they would have needed to be written in the first place: code, context, object, addressee, author. If we did this, would we have been "reading" the marks?

We would have made a sense *for* the marks, but would we have made sense *of* them? I think that our notion of reading depends upon some irreducible minimum of recuperation or centripetality in the process of generating meaning. Reading comes after writing. We must look backward and find something there in order to be reading at all. We must, in fact, have some hints or fragments of the code in which the text was composed for us to begin reading. Derrida seems at times to be denying this, as in the observation we just noted, which is one of the conclusions of *Sec*: "Writing is read; it is not the site . . . of a hermeneutic deciphering, the decoding of a meaning or truth" (*Limited Inc*, 21). Here, as elsewhere, Derrida asserts that any attempt to recuperate meaning from a text is equivalent to searching for a truth that could only be guaranteed by some impossible Platonic Absolute. I have no desire to challenge the antimetaphysical (and therefore metaphysical) part of Derrida's program. But I wonder why, in the terms used by Derrida himself, *meaning* must be equated with *truth*? This equation, "meaning *or* truth," simply begs the question under discussion. That is, the equation suppresses any possible difference between *meaning* and *truth*, ignoring, for instance, the existence of meaningful lies. Beyond that, there are serious problems in the extension of the attack on metaphysical truth to the more mundane aspects of reading and writing, including literary criticism and interpretation. Specifically, when it comes to reading, I can accept the Derridean point that a pure or perfect recuperation of a text is both theoretically and practically impossible. There is no such thing as an ideal reading. The question remains, however, as to what conclusions ought to be drawn from the impossibility of an ideal or perfect reading. I contend that "hermeneutic deciphering" is alive and well in most Derridean practice, though disparaged openly by Derrida and his American followers. Deconstruction as a mode of critical discourse is not an alternative to hermeneutics but an addition or corrective to it. We can see this when we consider Derrida's own reaction to being read.

We have before us in "Limited Inc a b c . . ." his response to being read by John Searle. We might expect him to be, as we say, philosophical about it and accept misreading along with *différance* (and original sin, which it closely resembles) as the fate of readers and writers doomed to iterability in this world—but no, iterability yields all too readily to irritability, and Derrida calls in what he refers to when others invoke it as the "language-police," just as any property owner calls the cops when a burglar arrives. Reading Searle's reading of *Sec*, Derrida observes that neither Searle nor anyone else can "be expected to know something which although outside of *Sec*, still forms part of its context. But whoever accepts the convention that consists in saying that one is going to read and criticize *Sec* is required to read what, within its limited corpus, points toward this context" (*Limited Inc*, 104). He is of course wittily using speech act notions against Searle, here, turning the intruder's own weapons against him, but this use still betrays or undoes the deconstructive view of reading. It is notably undeconstructive, for instance, to insist that "whoever accepts the convention that . . . one is going to read and criticize *Sec* is *required* to read" something. We are some distance from "dissemination" here. In fact, this looks like a classic case of whose ox is being gored—or rather whose text is being read.

In the case of Derrida, we can find frequent instances of sympathy for the outlaw becoming righteous indignation when his own textual property is at stake. We need look only at certain pages of *Critical Inquiry* to find him adopting both positions. In the issue called *On Narrative* (vol. 7, no. 1) we find a Derridean discussion of "The Law of Genre," which is a celebration of the violation of generic "law" by Maurice Blanchot in a text entitled *La Folie du jour*. Derrida predictably demonstrates that the concept of "law" inevitably implicates "lodged within the heart of law itself, a law of impurity or a principle of contamination" (57). Following this line of thought, Derrida argues that texts may participate in one or more genres, yet such participation "never amounts to belonging" (65). If one could assign a text to a genre with certainty, one could limit the readings of the text to those appropriate to the assigned genre. The genre is always on the side of law, and law on the side of genre. However, it is impossible to assign anything to any category, according to deconstructive logic; therefore, genres can set no limits to reading. This is not news (except, perhaps, in Chicago), but it sits awkwardly, to say the least, with a statement such as the following, drawn from Derrida's response to two critics in *Critical Inquiry*:

> What I, on the other hand, must recall to your attention—and I will remind you of it more than once—is that the text of an *appeal* obeys certain rules; it has its grammar, its rhetoric, its pragmatics. I'll come back to this point in a moment, to wit: as you did not take these rules into account, you quite simply *did not read* my text, in the most elementary and quasi-grammatical sense of what is called *reading*. ["But, beyond . . . ," 157]

What Derrida says here, through his obvious pain and outrage at being misread, is that reading involves some observation of the generic and contextual features involved in the production of a text. I could not agree more, and I believe he has always understood this and given many indications that this was his position. But he has also and more visibly adopted positions that seemed to suggest the opposite, calling for a freedom and play in reading and interpretation that allowed many of his American followers to ignore a significant conservatism in his views on these matters.

It is perhaps unfortunate that this conservatism emerges most vigorously when his own texts are being read, but few of us are in a position to throw stones about this type of behavior. The really sacred texts are the ones we write ourselves. Hermeneutics begins at home. The issue here is not this touch of human fallibility in an intellectual leader but what his followers ought to make of it. It is not a question of whether Derrida practices what he preaches, but of what should be made of this gap between theory and practice by those who are concerned with practice themselves, and particularly those concerned with the teaching of a certain practice of reading and writing. I wish to invite those individuals, teachers of reading and writing who have found or hope to find guidance or stimulation in the work of Derrida, to look more closely with me at his practice in *Sec* and its associated texts, for here he addresses most directly the practice of human communication.

Sec itself, even before Searle's intervention, was not just a "dry" exposition of theory but practice of a particular sort: a contest, a struggle not only with the named antagonist, J. L. Austin, but also with one who is not named, whose presence is invoked not by his name but by its absence, an absence that is marked by a systematic movement through the features of communication as he described and popularized them. I refer, of course, to Roman Jakobson. I am not going to defend Jakobson's property or his copyright, nor yet deny the interest and importance of Derrida's critique. I am concerned with use, primarily. As a teacher of language and literature—or, better, of textuality—I am interested in the possible uses of any theory of communication. I am also interested in the claims to truth or validity made by such theories—and I must confess to a spectatorial fascination with the agon itself. The intellectual coming to grips of Derrida and Searle, with Richard Rorty and others gradually being drawn in, attracts me as in itself interesting, as well as shedding light on questions of practical importance to my function as a teacher.

It is easy enough to show that when the issue is a struggle for power and position—and the four texts through which Derrida and Searle have come to grips (that is, the two by Derrida, Searle's reply to *Sec* in *Glyph* 1, and his review of *On Deconstruction*) are certainly that among other things—the contestants constantly resort to authority, to forceful language. The following statements, with the names replaced by letters, reveal a charming similarity:

> 1. *X has a distressing penchant for saying things that are obviously false.*
>
> 2. *When Y arrives at context, it is to say things that would be simply trivial were they not above all dubious.*

In this equation, and it is an equation, X = false and Y = dubious— and I take *dubious* to be a euphemism for *false* uttered by someone who has abandoned the true/false dichotomy but wants to use it all the same, so Y = false, also. Therefore $X = Y$ and I have proved by algebra that Searle and Derrida are the same. Q.E.D. (Derrida, catching himself using the word *false* in "Limited Inc a b c . . . " claims to have been infected by Searle's prose.)

They are also, of course, different, and it is Derrida's difference that interests me here: his difference from Searle, to be sure, but more importantly, his difference from himself. It interests me that Derrida regularly (and long before he read Searle) resorts to euphemisms that invoke the true/false dichotomy without naming it, as in the question he poses in *Sec* about the concept of context: "Is there a rigorous and scientific concept of *context*?" (*Limited Inc*, 3). "Rigorous and scientific" here must refer to some criteria of truth-value or logical validity to which Derrida, however implicitly, subscribes, but the role of "rigor" in Derrida's theory of reading is a matter to which we shall return later in this chapter.

In the struggle with a critical antagonist, we find Derrida, like the rest of us, resorting to the "language-police," to science, rigor, or other euphemisms for the Law which he sometimes affects to be above—or below. But this struggle is not—for Derrida in particular—a special case of discourse. Much of his best writing has taken the form of commentary that becomes contest. I think here not only of the series of boxing matches that constitutes *Of Grammatology*—first sparring with Saussure, learning the moves, then a quick knockout of Lévi-Strauss (using a low blow, however, by revealing how Lévi-

Strauss fictionalized his more authentic dissertation), followed by a gruelling decision over Rousseau, ending with both fighters, and the spectators, exhausted—but also of the loving, patient wrestling matches with Husserl's theory of signs and essay on the origin of geometry, as well as the judo contest with Lacan over Poe's "Purloined Letter."

"Limited Inc a b c . . ." is obviously a no-holds-barred battle with Searle, but its predecessor, *Sec*, was a struggle for power and position before Searle intervened at all: not merely a contest with Austin or with Jakobson but an argument over philosophical space. Derrida takes the common notion that writing is a type of communication and turns it around to assert that communication is a type of writing. Considered spatially the contest can be described in terms of whether writing is within a larger entity called communication, or communication is contained by some arche-writing. This is a struggle with all sorts of political and economic implications. All of Derrida's jokes about copyright and property in "Limited Inc a b c . . . " are an index of his own investment in the takeover of the Communications Corp. (or core or corps or corpus or corpse) by Writing Unlimited, J. Derrida, Prop.

The political and economic implications extend far beyond the individuals who have constructed the texts in question. Derrida's position is often presented, by himself as well as others, as opposed to law, authority, and power as these exist in various institutional structures. The source of his appeal—without denying the fascination of his writing *as writing*—for American academicians is partly to be found in this political attitude. In particular, for the generation whose sensibilities were shaped by the 1960s, the anarchistic irreverence of deconstruction holds a profound attraction. For those who still remember the slogans of the past well enough to think of themselves as having sold out, as having been co-opted by the establishment, the verbal or textual posture offered by deconstructive discourse is almost irresistible. Its appeal is so strong because it allows a displacement of political activism into a textual world where anarchy can *become* the establishment without threatening the actual seats of political and economic power. Political radicalism may thus be drained off or sublimated into a textual radicalism that can happily theorize its own disconnection from unpleasant realities.

The therapeutic effect of all this is far too obvious for anyone to condemn it outright. It does people good to feel radical and go around deconstructing things. And it is possible, as many writers have shown, to adapt the methodology of deconstructive analysis to secular or political ends. However, to use deconstruction and, above all, to teach it, we must ask of it the questions Derrida asks of the positions he, himself, questions. To use his own terminology, we can ask whether the position he develops in *Sec* is "rigorous and scientific" or "dubious." It seems to me to be an interesting mixture of the rigorous and the dubious. One might well leave matters there were it not that Derrida's whole enterprise is based upon exposing the imperfection or impurity of other people's terminology. If a concept is not "pure" (one of his favorite words) it can be degraded or discarded. In *Sec* he brings charges of imperfection against the concepts of *code* and *context*. Of *context* he asks the question, "Is there a rigorous and scientific concept of *context*?" His answer is that he "shall try to demonstrate why a context is never absolutely determinable, or rather, why its determination can never be certain or saturated" (*Limited Inc*, 3).

This is the basic position in most of his critical arguments, a position that has been found philosophically absurd by Searle and also by Richard Rorty, who recently observed, "Searle is, I think, right in saying that a lot of Derrida's arguments (not to mention some of Nietzsche's) are just awful. He is very acute in remarking that many of them depend upon the assumption that 'unless a distinction can be made rigorous and precise it isn't really a distinction at all'" ("Deconstruction and Circumvention," 22*n*). Calling in the Purity-Police, as Derrida does regularly, is not only a dubious action for someone who claims the status of outlaw but also an absurd form of argument—and can be shown to be such.

The concept of purity is, of course, dependent upon its opposite, impurity, for definition. We apply the word *pure* only to that which may possibly be impure. In deconstructive terms, this means that the concept of purity contains within it traces of its anticoncept, impurity. As Derrida puts it in "Limited Inc," "if a certain 'break' is always possible, that with which it breaks must necessarily bear the mark of this possibility inscribed within its structure. This is the thesis of *Sec*" (*Limited Inc*, 64). Thus purity bears the trace of impurity "inscribed within its structure." From this point one can go in two directions, both of which are bad for Derrida's enterprise. *Either* this contaminated concept of purity is now rendered useless because it is uncertain or unreliable, deficient in science and rigor. *Or* concepts don't need to be pure in order to be used in a rigorous argument, in which case he has no case against those he criticizes. The now classic deconstructionist response to this situation is to use the impure terms "under erasure," which means that one doesn't subscribe to or believe in the system of meaning that supports such terms but must use them because they are all we have and it is better to speak out than to remain silent. One can be sympathetic to this position—despite Wittgenstein's powerful silence arguing the contrary—but even so it is hard not to feel that rigor is banished from any discourse that will condemn a term when used by others but then turn right around and use it to perform critical work.

In *Sec*, for instance, Derrida dismisses the concept of *code* just as he had dismissed that of *context*: "I prefer not to become too involved here with this concept of code which does not seem very reliable to me" (*Limited Inc*, 10). The unreliability or uncertainty of the concept of code, however, does not prevent Derrida from calling in the code-police in "Limited Inc" to arrest Searle for missing a particular intended signification in *Sec*: "*Sec* uses/mentions the code of traditional philosophy (among others); one of its conventions . . . supposes the knowledge of certain *a b c*s of classical philosophy, so that when it uses or mentions the word 'modification,' it is also to signify modal determination" (*Limited Inc*, 100). To read *Sec* properly, or seriously, one must know the codes it uses. So says Jacques Derrida. He also, and this is perhaps more interesting, speaks on behalf of the author's intention, though he tries to employ a syntactic form that will allow him to do this by a ventriloquial process: "when *it* uses or mentions . . . *it* is also *to signify*." Surely intention is at stake in this utterance. Derrida would have it that *Sec*—that is, the text, the writing—is the agent in this case. It is *Sec* that uses or mentions. But can anyone doubt that it is Derrida's own authorial amour propre that animates his defense of the intention and the codes of the text that bears his signature? Derrida will hasten to tell us, of course, that intentions are never pure or certain: "Intention is a priori (at once) *différante*: differing and deferring, in its inception" (*Limited Inc*, 56). No argument—but what follows from our knowing this? That we should read without regard for intention? I have two answers to this question. First, I see no way to get "rigorously" from the impurity of intention in theory to the disregard of it in practice. Second, if we look at what Derrida does, as opposed to what he says, he reads others with regard to their intentions and he obviously wants to be read that way himself.

The question of intention brings us to what seems to me the most dubious dimension of Derrida's discussion of communication in *Sec* and his earlier discussions of writing and speech. In *Sec* this doubtfulness or unreliability emerges most clearly in his discussion of the "subject" of utterance: the one who says "I." As soon as this matter is raised in *Sec*, Derrida shifts from speech to writing, from the one who says "I" to the written signature, insisting that there is no significant difference between the two:

Let us attempt to analyze signatures, their relation to the present and to the source. I shall consider it as an implication of the analysis that every predicate established will be equally valid for that oral "signature" constituted—or aspired to—by the presence of the "author" as a "person who utters," as a "source," to the production of the utterance. [*Limited Inc*, 20]

Derrida will "consider" that what he says about written signatures will also hold for the oral 'signature,' "—for saying "I"—because speech and writing are, in every respect that matters, the same. They are the same because they are both marked by *différance*, and everything marked by *différance* is a kind of writing.

In the case of written signatures, Derrida asks whether a signature marks an event in the past, at which the one who signed was actually present to write the signature. His answer to this question is that a signature could be connected to its source only if certain conditions were perfectly fulfilled: "In order for the tethering to the source to occur, what must be retained is the absolute singularity of a signature-event and a signature-form: the pure reproducibility of a pure event" (*Limited Inc*, 20). Here come the purity-police again. They will demonstrate—as they always do—that the object in question has impurity inscribed within its structure. In this case, the possibility of functioning as a signature entails (a priori) the impossibility of so functioning: "In order to function, that is, to be readable, a signature must have a repeatable, iterable, imitable form; it must be able to be detached from the present and singular intention of its production. It is its sameness which, by corrupting its identity and its singularity, divides its seal" (ibid.).

It is the very readability of a signature—or any other sign—that is the measure of its *différance*. Signs are always both the same as and different from whatever they may have been at their moment of origin. So runs the argument. We should be aware, of course, that this is a version of Derrida's most persistent and consequential argument, which makes the same case with respect to perception that is made here with respect to reading. Since we can never perceive perfectly the absolute whole of anything instantaneously, all perception is impure, a reading of signs rather than an apprehension of things. The condition of reading is the human condition.

This is a case I am entirely willing to grant. But I do not see how we get from this discussion of absolutes to any practical conclusions. If everything in our world is impure, insofar as we know anything about it, this means that purity is not a concept that we can use, except in a relative way, more or less pure, more or less impure. Similarly, if none of us ever experiences the pure presence of anything, then we can stop talking about pure presence as if it mattered. In order to speak at all we must acknowledge that we are talking about degrees of things, including those things that Derrida uses as absolute terms of value: rigor, science, certainty, reliability, and the like. Derrida continues to argue, however, in the Afterword to *Limited Inc*, that philosophical concepts must be presented within a "logic of all or nothing": "Every concept which lays claim to any rigor whatsoever implies the alternative 'all or nothing.'" At the same time he insists that his own special terminology—"when I speak of *différance*, of mark, of supplement, of iterability and of all they entail"—can be positioned outside this all or nothing logic simply because he has made "explicit in the most conceptual, rigorous, formalizing and pedagogical manner the reasons one has for doing so, for thus changing the rules and the context of discourse" (*Limited Inc*, 116–17). Frankly, I do not believe that he has actually done or can actually accomplish any such thing. That is, I do not believe that one can rigorously, logically explain why one's own terminology need not be rigorous and logical while other people's must be. In his essay *"Différance"* (English version in *Speech and Phenomena*), Derrida asserts repeatedly that *différance* is neither a word nor a concept, but this is a mere assertion rather than a rigorous demonstration—for the very good reason that the existence of a word that is not a word or a concept that is not a concept cannot be demonstrated within a rigorous logic, since this constitutes a paradox, and logic cannot accept paradoxes. This notion also contradicts the deconstructive principle that we perceive only signs. As Eliot's Sweeney says, "I've gotta use words when I talk to you." By the end of Derrida's essay on the subject, whatever it may have been before, *différance* is clearly both a word and a concept, subject to the same problematic of iterability as every other sign.

In short, Derrida's critique of concepts like "presence" is based upon a set of terms that have been specifically exempted from this very sort of critique. Therefore, we are perfectly justified in questioning this critique and employing the concept for our own pragmatic ends, accepting his general injunction to think about these matters as rigorously as we can. We shall return to this word *rigor* itself a bit later on, but first we must reconsider briefly the notion of presence. Presence is important because the distinction between speech and writing is based, to a great extent, upon that very notion. And this distinction, I wish to argue, is one that students of language and literature cannot afford to neglect.

Before developing this final point of my examination of Derrida's critique of communication, let me say that I have no special attachment to vocalized speech, to sound itself. Most of what I have to say would apply at least as well to any developed sign language. But I believe there is a crucial difference between signs exchanged by people who are present to one another and in the presence of the objects of their speech, and signs that function in other ways. One of those crucial differences is that we all learn the first elements of language through communication with another person in the presence of objects that can be named. I am reminded forcibly of this when my neighbor Brad, who is approaching his third birthday, comes over for a visit. Much of his speech takes the form of "What's that?" with the aid of a pointing finger.

I cannot imagine that Derrida wants to deny that we learn language in this way, depending on the presence of interlocutors to one another and the presence of objects to both of them. What he does want to deny is that anything is ever fully, purely, absolutely, instantaneously present to anybody. He believes that if we grant this we will have no rigorous ground for distinguishing between presence and absence. He would consider the notion of presence that I have been using both trivial and dubious, which is what he calls similar notions of Searle's. I would argue, however, that the notion of presence is so fundamental to language that, far from being some metaphysical trick foisted on language by philosophy, it is the constitutive possibility of language itself. This, in effect, is what Emile Benveniste has said in his well-known discussion of subjectivity in language:

Language is possible only because each speaker sets himself up as a *subject* by referring to himself as *I* in his discourse. Because of this, *I* posits another person, the one who, being, as he is, completely exterior to "me," becomes my echo to whom I say *you*, and who says *you* to me. This polarity of persons is the fundamental condition in language, of which the process of communication, in which we share, is only a mere pragmatic consequence. [Benveniste, 225]

Less well known but equally relevant to our inquiry is Bertrand Russell's discussion of what he calls "egocentric particulars" in human language. For Russell, words like *this, I,* and *now* have only a trivial signification apart from the occasion of their use. We may take *this* to mean the object of attention at a given moment; however, "many objects on many occasions are present to attention, but on each occasion only one is *this*" (Russell, 109). We have no access to the non-trivial meaning of *this* unless we also have access to the occasion of its use. Thus the trivial part of the signification of *this* is repeatable, but the nontrivial part is unique to its occasion. The understanding of such words is dependent on presence (presence to attention, as Russell says) and therefore tied to context. Russell is not as interested in the dialogical dimension of language as Benveniste, for whom the fact that "I" and "you" shift back and forth between interlocutors is crucial. But Russell's "egocentric particulars" and Benveniste's "shifters" pose a problem that the Derridean view of language largely ignores: not the problem of metaphysical presence but the problem of pragmatic presence, which is embedded in both the way we learn language and the way we use it.

Derrida, of course, would hold that what I am calling pragmatic presence is just the vulgar version of metaphysical presence. He has tried to demonstrate, with arguments that he admits obtain their own rigor from the metaphysical tradition, that presence and perception never actually occur. I admire the elegance of his demonstration, and to a certain extent find it persuasive, but I do not see how it leads to any useful conclusions. If we are perpetually denied any degree of presence and perception, surely we would be living under the regime of a negative Absolute, a nihilism in which, as Hegel said of Fichte's positive Absolute, is like "the night in which, as the saying goes, all cows are black." Derrida's view of reading seems to me—up to a point—decidedly nihilistic. But it also contains a distinct counterimpulse, in his practice and in his reactions to being read, as we have noticed, but also at certain points in his theoretical discussions. Before turning to this, however, we must finish examining the problems that arise in his theory of interpretation because of his denial of presence.

In *Sec*, as we have noted, Derrida substitutes the written signature for the spoken word "I," but in *Speech and Phenomena* (chap. 7, especially 93–97) he situates himself against a discussion of Husserl's that is very like Russell's treatment of "egocentric particulars": a discussion of words that, in Husserl's phrase, "orient actual meaning to the occasion, the speaker, and the situation" (quoted by Derrida, 93). These "occasional" expressions, which are essentially the same as Russell's "egocentric particulars," are treated by Derrida in a perfunctory, almost derisory, way, which is far different from most of this closely argued text. There are many things to be inferred from this, one of which is that we have here one of the weakest points in Derrida's theory of language. His tactic on this occasion is to let the word *I* stand for all the others (a matter that is far from justifiable, since the problems of *I* are not the same as the problems of *this*) and to argue that we always understand the *meaning* of "I" as "whatever speaker is designating himself," even if we do not know who utters the word. In short, he claims that what Russell called the "trivial" sense of the word is the only sense that counts.

The weakness of this position is masked well in its context by Derrida's conspicuous skill at shifting an argument onto favorable ground, but the problems remain all the same. A considerable amount of Derrida's early work is devoted to demonstrating that we are no more present to one another when we speak than when we put a message in a bottle and cast it upon the waters. Put this way, of course, it sounds absurd. Put Derrida's way—that we are never really, wholly, purely in a relationship that could be rigorously called "presence"—it sounds much more plausible and is perhaps more than plausible. My argument, however, is that no matter how plausible the case for impurity of presence may be, it does not alter the fact that pragmatic presence is a crucial dimension of language and that understanding and teaching about language depends upon our ability to speak of varying degrees or dimensions of presence and absence. To borrow Hegel's image, we need to talk about cows with different degrees of spottiness. The Derridean theory of language is usually deployed as if the critique of metaphysical presence was relevant—and damaging — to the notion of pragmatic presence: pragmatic presence being the sense in which, when you tell your child "*that* is a cat," the baby, the animal, and you are all present to one another. I have been arguing that pragmatic presence is essential to language and that this presence is marked by the features of language that Benveniste, Russell, and Husserl have brought to our attention. I hope to take the issue further, however, by showing that the Derridean theory of language is weakened by certain other problems.

Surely one of the most striking features of the theory of grammatology is the claim that the fallibility of human perception may be described in terms of writing, that is, in terms of a *différance* which is the structuring principle of both writing and perception. Humans have acquired language because the human perception of the world has always been enabled by, and marked by, the *différance* that assumes increasingly graphic forms throughout human history. In this view consciousness itself is a product of *différance* rather than a producer of differences—or, better, human consciousness is a producer of differences *because* it is a product of *différance* and marked by it from the beginning.

This elegant formulation has all the power of its history, which, as Derrida well knows, extends back to the pre-Socratics. From this perspective, human beings became human by receiving the gift of signs—at the cost of perceiving nothing but signs, everywhere. To be conscious—and, above all, to be conscious that one is conscious—is to be split, differentiated, alienated. All this, I think, we must grant, but separation and alienation are not the whole story of human consciousness. As Saussure makes clear many times and in many ways, language is not a random aggregation of differences but a *system* of distinctions. This systematic or integral quality of language is just as important as its differential quality. Linguistic signs are not simply differentiated; they are linked in patterns we have learned to call paradigmatic and deployed in patterns we call syntactic. It seems to me self-evident that the primordial source of linkage, pattern, and system cannot be adequately described in terms of *différance*, trace, and the other differential concepts generated by Derrida's nihilistic theory.

I am suggesting that Derrida's view of language is inadequate because it largely ignores the systematic quality of grammar and syntax. It should also be noted, however, that when he does turn his attention to these matters it is to characterize them as "linear" and to pose them invidiously in a binary opposition with a "pluri-dimensional" language that presumably transcends the linear order of human utterance as we know it. This view of language is developed in that section of the *Grammatology* devoted to the history of writing, called "Science and the Name of Man." In these pages Derrida follows in a manner far from critical the observations of André Leroi-Gourhan in his book *Le Geste et la parole* (1965). What is most striking about Derrida's presentation of the history of writing is that in it he subscribes to something suspiciously like a myth of lost linguistic plenitude, displayed in a binary opposition that takes the form of pluridimensionality versus linearity. This is important enough for us to examine it with some care:

> Writing in the narrow sense—and phonetic writing above all—is rooted in a past of non-linear writing. It had to be defeated, and here one can speak, if one wishes, of technical success; it assured a greater security and greater possibilities of capitalization in a dangerous and anguishing world. But that was not done *one single time*. A war was declared, and the suppression of all that resisted linearization was installed. And first of what Leroi-Gourhan calls the "mythogram," a writing that spells its symbols pluri-dimensionally; there the meaning is not subjected to successivity, to the order of logical time, or to the irreversible temporality of sound. This pluri-dimensionality does not paralyze history within simultaneity, it corresponds to another level of historical significance, and one may just as well consider, conversely, linear thought as a reduction of history. [*Grammatology*, 85, italics in original]

The translation here, though accurate enough, lacks its customary elegance, being faithful to a clumsiness of expression that overtakes the original at this point. One senses embarrassment all around, for here Derrida subscribes to a myth of the "mythogram," the discourse of a plenitude, an Eden of language, violated repeatedly (more than *"one single time"*) by the storm troopers of "linearity," who suppressed everything that resisted the technocratic, capitalistic onslaught of linearization. The astounding clumsiness of Derrida's prose in the quoted passage, marked especially by excessive use of passive constructions, is a sign of the embarrassment that has overtaken his discourse at this moment. *Someone* has declared war, put in motion a genocidal strategy against the mythogram and its adherents: "a war was declared . . . a suppression . . . was installed." Even as metaphor, this simply will not do. But this is not the whole story.

This mythic nostalgia for a lost plenitude of language is extended by

Derrida in a predictably linear and circular way to the present moment (which we should note is a moment in the 1960s), in which he himself functions as the precursor of a revived mythogramous culture, destined to emerge from the now decadent evil empire of linearity. We are to rejoice (or perhaps reJoyce) because of the "massive reappearance of non-linear writing":

This night [the Dark Ages of linear domination—otherwise known as the Enlightenment, or science] begins to lighten a little at the moment when linearity—which is not loss or absence but the repression of pluri-dimensional symbolic thought—relaxes its oppression because it begins to sterilize the technical and scientific economy that it has too long favored. In fact for a long time its possibility has been bound up with that of economy and technics, and of ideology. This solidarity appears in the process of thesaurization, capitalization, sedentarization, hierarchization, of the formation of ideology by the class that writes or rather commands the scribes. [*Grammatology*, 86]

In these pages we have surely found what Derrida has taught us to think of as a textual blind spot. This is not simply an aberration caused by the philosopher straying into history. This aberration is necessary. Because Derrida sees language as essentially differential—the product of a purely divisive force that has shaped consciousness in its own image—he must find in history some actual language that corresponds to his view. And this is exactly what he finds, only it is situated in a mythic past, the inconceivable "before" of the mythogram, and in an equally mythic future, which is nevertheless at hand:

What is thought today cannot be written according to the line and the book, except by imitating the operation implicit in teaching modern mathematics with an abacus. This inadequation is not *modern*, but it is exposed today better than ever before. The access to pluri-dimensionality and to a delinearized temporality is not a simple regression toward the "mythogram"; on the contrary, it makes all the rationality subjected to the linear model appear as another form and another age of mythography. The meta-rationality of the meta-scientificity which are thus announced within the meditation upon writing can therefore be no more shut up within a science of man than conform to the traditional idea of science. In one and the same gesture, they leave *man, science,* and the *line* behind. [*Grammatology*, 87]

Perhaps the kindest thing one can say about this is that in the two decades since it was written the movement toward metarationality has not progressed much, but kindness itself would be impertinent on this occasion. These "metas" beg too many questions, as, indeed, does Derrida's whole attempt to think writing historically on the basis of a view of language as a purely differential and differentiating activity. Even a "meta-rationality" requires a *ratio*, and that is precisely what *différance* alone could never achieve.

The inadequacies I have mentioned in Derrida's view of language (the impossibility of using the concept of purity rigorously; the inadequate treatment of shifters or egocentric particulars; an inability to account for the systematic quality of language; and a historical view of writing that is both thin and marred by the myth of the mythogram) should make us wary of accepting that view as the ground upon which a theory of communication—and in particular a theory of reading—might be based. We have also noticed an apparent disparity between Derrida's theory of reading as presented in *Sec* and his own reactions to being read—or misread. But do we know what theory of reading he is actually proposing in his early writings? There is some evidence on the question in *Of Grammatology* and *Positions* that we should attend to before concluding.

In *Of Grammatology* the crucial passage is the section called "The Exorbitant Question of Method" (157–64). These pages repay the most careful study and discussion, and I shall inevitably do them some violence in summarization here. In them Derrida argues that critical reading does not recapitulate a meaning that is already given in a text but produces a new signifying structure. Yet this signifying structure should not be entirely new, for it must be produced in part through a traditional method—"the effaced and respectful doubling of commentary"—which, Derrida tells us, "should no doubt have its place in a critical reading. To recognize and respect all its classical exigencies is not easy and requires all the instruments of traditional criticism. Without this recognition and this respect, critical production would risk developing in any direction at all and authorize itself to say almost anything" (*Grammatology*, 158). It is clear that Derrida recoils here from some anarchy of readers, producing, perhaps, Eskimo interpretations of "A Rose for Emily." The traditional methods of tex-

tual exegesis are not to be discarded. But—and it is a large "But"—
these methods are only of negative value, a "guardrail" that will keep
one on the right track. They will not take us anywhere new: "this
indispensable guardrail has always only *protected*, it has never *opened*, a
reading" (158, emphasis in original). A critical reading must indeed get
somewhere, must open some new perspective on the text read, and
not simply double or repeat the text respectfully. It must be exorbitant
and to be so it must be, in a sense, disrespectful. This, I believe, is
where the *critical* in "critical reading" enters the process. This textual
activity both includes recuperation and exceeds it in some way—but
not just in any way.

Derrida prudently refuses to define the way critical reading should
be practiced—except negatively—but he clearly offers his own critical
readings of Saussure, Lévi-Strauss, and Rousseau as examples of
how it may be done. He very definitely cares about what makes good
reading good, but he does not wish to make explicit—or feels unable
to make explicit—exactly what the principles of good reading ought
to be. Such reading must be exorbitant—but it should not be free. He
says as much again in *Positions*: "These texts are not to be read according to a hermeneutical or exegetical method which would seek out a
finished signified beneath a textual surface. Reading is transformational. . . . But this transformation cannot be executed however one
wishes. It requires protocols of reading" (63). Derridean reading is
not, then, a matter of free play. One cannot do it "however one
wishes." In fact, there must be rules of interpretive transformation:
"protocols of reading." Of such protocols, however, Derrida says
bluntly, "I have not yet found any that satisfy me." There must be
rules—but there are no rules. What is it, then, that checks or guides
our exegetical transformation or critical reading? What makes a reading rigorously exorbitant rather than simply idiosyncratic or naive?
Derrida will not or cannot say. But what is inexplicit is not necessarily
absent. There is a code in place that governs Derrida's own practice as
a reader, and one of the tasks of a critical reading of his work must be
to discover and describe as fully as possible that code. For, at the
moment, if he has offered us a theory of reading, it is a theory with a
gap in its most crucial place. What belongs in that gap, along with a
few other matters, will be the subject of the rest of this chapter.

What I am undertaking here is a "reading" of Derrida that is largely centripetal rather than centrifugal or exorbitant. That is, I am mainly engaged here in the respectful doubling of commentary. However, since my way of reading his intent will require that I say at times what he does not say, this reading will inevitably have a centrifugal dimension as well. In his important and interesting response to Gerald Graff's questions in the Afterword to *Limited Inc*, Derrida has himself reread the chapter on "The Exorbitant Question of Method" from *Of Grammatology* and amplified the position that we have just been discussing. In this comment on his own text he makes a number of crucial points about reading. To begin with he amplifies what he meant by what he called in the earlier text, "perhaps clumsily," as he says, "doubling commentary," indicating both his acceptance of what I have called the centripetal dimension of reading and his belief that no reading can ever be purely centripetal: that commentary can never fully double an original text, no matter how respectful it intends to be. But we should consider his own words on this important question. The moment of doubling commentary, he says,

does not suppose the self-identity of "meaning" but a relative stability of the dominant interpretation (including the "self"-interpretation) of the text being commented upon. With, as I say in this passage, all the "classical exigencies" and the "instruments of traditional criticism" (of which, by the way, I thereby indicate, in a political-institutional proposition, the vital necessity. the university should, I believe, assure the most rigorous transmission and conservation, but the best strategy to this end is never simple), "doubling commentary" is not a moment of simple reflexive recording that would transcribe the originary and true layer of a text's intentional meaning, a meaning that is univocal and self-identical, a layer upon which or after which active interpretation would finally begin. [*Limited Inc*, 143]

Let me say at once that I entirely agree with these words, not just in their large implications but in their nuances as well. One cannot achieve a good centripetal reading without some necessary admixture of the centrifugal. One cannot, that is, ever be fully respectful, since respect requires a certain amount of opposition. In the present case, I shall be reading Derrida himself in the light of my own concerns, and my method will involve positioning his view of reading against that of a philosopher of very different background. I shall also be "breaking up" Derrida's texts, in pursuit of a single crucial word that is both indispensable to his thinking and, at a certain point, in a certain way, is the mark of a weak spot in the Derridean theory of reading.

I shall first of all position Derrida's views against those of a contemporary Platonist (rare creature) who has studied with both Leo Strauss and Alexandre Kojève (and written about both of them as well). This philosopher is Stanley Rosen, whom I have already cited as an opponent of contemporary nihilism. I put Rosen and Derrida together, in this case, not capriciously, but because the opposition of the two thinkers—along with some surprising affinities—will help in the complex project at hand: the articulation of a theory of reading by means of a reading of Derrida's theory of reading. I am also advocating this sort of procedure as a proper move in any critical reading. Comparison and contrast is not just some sort of academic reflex but a fundamental part of the reading process—which is to say, the thinking process.

We can begin reading in the present instance by looking at what Rosen and Derrida have said about the theory and practice of reading, considering first their positions on the possible relationships between hermeneutic theory and the practice of interpretation. In doing so we may be surprised to discover that their views on this matter seem to converge. We can begin by comparing the following statement by Rosen to Derrida's now familiar comment on the protocols of interpretation:

There are no canons by which one can usefully restrict legitimate from illegitimate readings. The reliance upon canons, apparently in opposition to the extreme relativism of the radical postmodernists, has the unfortunate consequence of trivializing the interpretation of works of genius. I see no reason to prefer conservative obtuseness to radical hypomania. . . . For my part, I prefer hypomania to canonical stultification. [Rosen, *Hermeneutics as Politics*, 143]

Derrida says that canons or protocols of reading are desirable but unlikely, if not impossible, of attainment. In practice, however, as we have just seen, he makes it clear that he accepts the traditional canons of interpretation and scholarship as necessary though insufficient for good practice in the reading of texts. Good practice, however, depends on going beyond the canons, on being "exorbitant." Rosen, on the other hand—well, Rosen does not seem to be on the other hand at all but on the very same hand as Derrida. He espouses "hypomania" or "divine madness," as he sometimes calls it, which I read as Derridean exorbitance plus the conviction of being inspired, and he specifically espouses this hypomania in opposition to those who suggest canons or protocols as a way of curbing postmodernist excess. Nihilists and Platonists apparently share a fondness for madness or extravagance and a distrust of methods and rules.

What both these philosophers share is an extreme skepticism about the value of canons or protocols of interpretation. But within that skepticism there remain some interesting differences. Rosen states his position (in the ellipsis I left in the above quotation) as follows:

> I would of course not deny that it is possible to write down on a sheet of paper prudential maxims to be followed by all competent readers. But competent readers do not require such a list, and its possession does not transform incompetence into competence. More seriously, it does not enable us to cross the bar from the commonsensical to the domain of divine madness. Instead, it empowers scholastic mediocrity to pose as the guardian of legitimate genius. [143]

Where Derrida sees prudential maxims as the "indispensable guardrail" for the best interpretive practice, Rosen sees them in much the way that Socrates saw writing: as empowering mediocrity to pose as wisdom. The crucial difference between Derrida and Rosen on this point involves the nature of competence itself. For Rosen, competence is not learned but innate, as his discussion of human nature makes plain.

In taking a position against historicism, Rosen argues, "If there is no human nature that remains constant within historical change, and so defines the perspectives of individual readers *as* perspectives upon a common humanity, then reading is impossible." This seems to me an important and far from trivial position. I must confess to some personal hesitation between historicist and essentialist positions on this question, which certainly needs further consideration. For the moment, however, what is important is not this large and consequential question but the way that Rosen slides from his assertion about the constancy of human nature in general to a quite different assertion about the constancy of individual human subjects: "We do not become subtle through the study of philology," he says. "To the contrary, only those who are subtle by nature will make an appropriate use of their philological training. And there are neither philological canons nor ontological definitions of subtlety" (146–47). Those who are born subtle are worthy of training. They are the elect. Those who are not, let them be hewers of wood and drawers of water, for their lack of subtlety is innate and essential, beyond the remedy of any teaching.

This is a hard doctrine, in which Calvin seems to have the upper hand over Plato. Leaving aside the question of its truth, it seems to me a doctrine very dangerous for a teacher to hold. Its weakest point, from this perspective, is the notion that subtlety—or the lack of it—is not only a permanent condition for each human being but an absolute one as well. One is either subtle or not, in this view, as one might be saved or damned, which leaves no room for degrees of subtlety and precious little for improvement. In this respect, Stanley Rosen, whose work I have admired and learned from over the years, comes very close to being what I would call a vulgar essentialist. Where Derrida stands on this question is perhaps less clear, but in any case the issue is not where these individuals stand but where we all should stand on the questions that have been dominating my discussion here: the question of the proper relationship between the theory and practice of interpretation, and the related question about the extent to which the best interpretive practice can be methodized or taught.

We have already noted Derrida's ambivalence on the matter of protocols or methodization of reading. It is time now to probe more deeply into his position on this matter by looking more closely at his practice as a reader: specifically, at certain moments of his own critical reading in which he judges or evaluates the practice of reading and writing, whether another's or his own. In doing this, I shall not be so much interested in his reasoned arguments as in his presuppositions, as indicated primarily by his adjectives and adverbs of judgment. This may seem like a perverse procedure, but I shall try to justify it by the result. We can begin by looking at some brief judgmental phrases, torn from their contexts for our analytical purposes. To aid in this analysis, I shall emphasize a crucial word that appears in all the excerpts:

FROM *SPEECH AND PHENOMENA:*

the **rigor** and subtlety of Husserl's analysis [4–5]

Our discussion ought to incorporate these protected nuances and thereby at the same time *consolidate in them its own possibility and rigor* [13–14, italics in original]

This takes form slowly, prudently, but **rigorously** in the *Investigations* [37]

under the surveillance of a differentiated, bold, and **rigorous** transcendental reduction [39]

without neglecting the novelty and **rigor** of the phenomenological description of images [54–55]

it is supposed that . . . a **rigorous** distinction can be drawn [56–57]

without being able here to follow the **rigorous** development of this text [64]

Does not this compromise . . . the **rigorous** separation of indication from expression? [68]

whatever the success and **rigor** of his analyses [71]

despite the minute detail, the **rigor**, and the absolute novelty of his analyses [81]

without disregarding the **rigor** and boldness of "pure logical grammar" [98]

FROM *OF GRAMMATOLOGY:*

it is necessary . . . to designate **rigorously** [14]

in order to reach the **rigorous** thought [23]

only then will one be able to state **rigorously** [46]

To think play radically the ontological and transcendental

problematics . . . must be patiently and **rigorously** worked through [50]

Without this reduction . . . the distinction . . . would have no **rigor** [53]

Even if this commonsensical proposition were **rigorously** proved [54]

Never . . . would a **rigorous** philosopher of consciousness have been so quickly persuaded [117]

It is possible to make them agree among themselves in the systematic **rigor** of conceptuality [18]

the system is articulated in the most **rigorous** and complete way [119]

A question that has meaning only through implying an original **rigor** in Marxist criticism [120]

There follows a distinction . . . which, some fifty years previously, a philosopher of consciousness, more neglected than others, had articulated **rigorously** [121]

it is difficult in any **rigorous** way to place the beginnings of science in the nineteenth century [130]

the empirical character of the analyses . . . removed all **rigor** from each of the propositions [131]

a consequence that cannot be **rigorously** deduced from these premises [132]

Only a [creationist] theology can sanction an essential and **rigorous** difference between the engineer and the *bricoleur* [139]

No model of reading seems to me at the moment ready to measure up to this text. . . . Measure up to it fully and **rigorously**, that is [149]

FROM *POSITIONS:*

I try to respect as **rigorously** as possible the internal, regulated play of philosophemes [6]

elucidating the relationship to Hegel . . . is interminable, at least if one wishes to execute it **rigorously** [44]

In each text, as can be verified, I constrain myself to act such that . . . what I consider to be *new* theoretical and indispensable premises . . . are not muddled by hasty inferences having no **rigorous** status [83]

there is no *effective* and *efficient* position . . . without a minute, **rigorous**, extended analysis [94]

It should be apparent, even in this hasty and far from rigorous assemblage of excerpts, how pervasive the notion of rigor is in Derrida's critical judgments. It is his major implement for criticizing the work of other thinkers—or for praising them—and it is a standard that he clearly holds before himself at all times. The word is also employed in his recent Afterword to *Limited Inc*, where it appears more than twenty times. And what is this rigor, to which he appeals so often? Without pretending to examine each use of this term carefully, let me hazard a few generalizations based on prolonged consideration of these texts. First of all, we can say that rigor is what Derrida uses to oppose the notion of truth as presence, truth as revelation; so that rigor, in this perspective, is the dark shadow of truth that haunts nihilistic hermeneutics. It is a virtue of method, of process, rather than of result, of product. Derrida associates this virtue, explicitly and consistently, with the practice of the critics of consciousness or phenomenologists, and in particular with the work of Edmund Husserl. Rigor is, par excellence, a philosopher's virtue. It is also, unlike Stanley Rosen's "subtlety," a virtue acquired by study and emulation, by socialization into a discourse. It belongs neither to theory nor to practice, exclusively, but to both. It is rigor that makes nihilistic hermeneutics a hermeneutics; while it is the absence of truth, or as Derrida would say (has said; see *Positions*, 105*n*), the presence of the idea of truth only as an indispensable fetish rather than an extratextual guarantee, that makes this hermeneutics nihilistic.

The concept of rigor dominates Derrida's recent discussion of reading in the Afterword to *Limited Inc*. In this important text he locates rigor as the force that sustains the logic of conceptual analysis "against all empirical confusion" but "also requires the structure of that logic to be transformed or complicated" (123). We should not pass over this too quickly. Traditional logic is itself the product of rigor and must therefore be "sustained." But rigor *requires* that we go beyond the structure of that logic. This "going beyond" is what Derrida has called deconstruction. Deconstruction, then, is not a renunciation of logic but a dialectical movement beyond logic a negation that preserves what it negates while transforming it, and this dialectic is driven not, like Hegel's dialectic, by the Absolute itself, but by Rigor—which I have written with a capital *R* to emphasize that it plays in Derrida's thought a role analogous to that of the Absolute in Hegel's. Rigor is Derrida's talisman against relativism and historicism, which he has regularly opposed and criticized. It is rigor that separates his position from that of Stanley Fish, Knapp and Michaels, and other vulgar nihilists. Rigor comes closer than any other term used by Derrida to being a protocol of reading. Still, attractive as this notion is, there are a number of problems attached to it that we must at least notice before closing this discussion. It can be so used, of course, only if it is itself outside the dialectic, beyond deconstruction—only, in short, if it is indeed an Absolute, functioning in much the same way as Reason has functioned in traditional philosophy. In this connection, we should note that Hilary Putnam has been arguing in recent years along lines that seem surprisingly convergent with Derrida's, which is to say that Putnam's views are becoming paradoxical, as we can see from the conclusion to "Why Reason Can't Be Naturalized": "If reason is both transcendent and immanent, then philosophy, as culture-bound re-flection and argument about eternal questions, is both in time and eternity. We don't have an Archimedean point; we always speak the language of a time and place; but the rightness and wrongness of what we say is not *just* for a time and a place" (Putnam, 247, italics in original).

Putnam's acceptance of the paradoxical may bring him closer to Derrida, as I have suggested, but his manner of locating his paradox clearly separates him from the French philosopher. His reason is reasonable because it is connected to some truth outside of time, like the *phronesis* of Aristotle, Gadamer, and Rosen, whereas Derrida's rigor is rigorous, apparently, in a purely formal or immanent manner and not because it transcends time and place. At least, that is how it appears, but it seems to me possible that Derridean rigor is just a mask for reason, another disguise of *phronesis* after all. I am convinced that without rigor as an ideal and as an embodied principle in Derrida's writing, that very writing would be far less interesting and important than it is. His rigor is not an ornament of rhetoric but a driving principle of the work, an aspect of the force that animates it. But if rigor is a good thing, and if it has remained much the same (or at least recognizable) from Plato's time to this, then perhaps it does indeed, to some extent, transcend time. As the guarantor or motivator of logic—and of whatever may allow logic to be "transformed or complicated"—it must partake of the onto-theo-logical to a greater extent than Derrida has admitted to us—or to himself. Nietzsche told us a century ago that "the nihilist does not believe that one needs to be logical" (*The Will to Power*, 18). The complete nihilist, I suspect, does not believe that one needs to be rigorous, either. If this premise is true, and if one is allowed to use logic after all, we have just found that Derrida cannot be a nihilist in any rigorous sense of that word. Since he denies the possibility of truth as reference, however, he cannot be a hermeneuticist, either. Yet he can, and does, practice a nihilistic hermeneutics. And so, I believe, do many of us at this point in our cultural history, though we have other names for our own varieties of interpretive practice, most of them vaguely honorific or self-congratulatory: names like "internal realism" or even "irrealism." Derrida belongs with this group. Like the others in it he stands opposed to relativism on the one hand and absolutism on the other. It is a difficult position to maintain, but it is the best available to us, as Leszek Kolakowski observed a few years ago, in concluding a series of lectures on Husserl:

> He [Husserl] better than anybody, compelled us to realize the painful dilemma of knowledge: either consistent empiricism, with its relativistic, skeptical results (a standpoint which many regard as discouraging, inadmissible, and in fact ruinous for culture) *or* transcendentalist dogmatism, which cannot really justify itself and remains in the end an arbitrary decision. I have to admit that although ultimate certitude is a goal that cannot be attained within the rationalist framework, our culture would be poor and miserable without people who keep trying to reach this goal, and it hardly could survive when left entirely in the hands of the skeptics. I do believe that human culture cannot ever reach a perfect synthesis of its diversified and incompatible components. Its very richness is supported by this very incompatibility of its ingredients. And it is the conflict of values, rather than their harmony, that keeps our culture alive. [Kolakowski, 85]

Kolakowski's return to Husserl should remind us that Husserl is where Derrida began and that his view of Husserl—and of our situation as readers—is in fact similar to Kolakowski's. It seems to me a very persuasive view. We have no choice but to read both rigorously and exorbitantly, centripetally and centrifugally at the same time, and, to the extent that we are teachers, to teach others to read in this way, too; which means, among other things, that we shall have to keep testing—in both theory and practice—the limits and possibilities of rigor and exorbitance. It is true, as Knapp and Michaels have claimed, that there is no place outside of practice where theory might stand in order to dictate protocols of reading—no Archimedean point, as Hilary Putnam put it. But there is no place outside of theory for practice to stand, either. Theory is not the superego of practice but its self-consciousness. The role of theory is not to lay down laws but to force us to be aware of what we are doing and why we are doing it. Practice without theory is blind, and in these dark times when nihilistic hermeneutics is the best we can do, we need all the light we can get. Though we may never be satisfied with our protocols, we must continue to construct—as well as deconstruct—them. This is true not only of interpretation but of criticism as well, where, as we shall see, a very similar dilemma awaits us.

Three

Criticism: Rhetoric and Ethics

Socrates, as we know, met the Sophists at every point, not by a bare reassertion of authority and tradition against their argumentations, but by showing dialectically how untenable the mere grounds were, and by vindicating the obligations of justice and goodness—by reinstating the universal or notion of the will. . . . Sophistry has nothing to do with what is taught: that may very possibly be true. Sophistry lies in the formal circumstance of teaching it by grounds which are as available for attack as for defence. In a time so rich in reflection and so devoted to *raisonnement* as our own, he must be a poor creature who cannot advance a good ground for everything, even for what is worst and most depraved. Everything in the world that has become corrupt has had good grounds for its corruption.

G. W. F. Hegel

Our distance from Hegel may perhaps be measured by the reluctance of our most subtle and rigorous thinkers to accept any universal or absolute as demonstrable by textual means. Derrida, like Nietzsche in his aphorism about the death of God, has simply expressed what was being thought around him, though his formulation has an impressive air of clarity and conviction. The absolute, says Derrida, is outside textuality—but there is no outside to textuality. Therefore, the absolute is nothing, or *différance*, a nonconcept too elusive for any universal to rest upon it. If the confrontation between Sophist and Socratist keeps returning to haunt us, the Sophist seems to have better lines on each return. The problem is that these lines are still not good enough. If Sophist and Socratist each tried to generate an ethic—the Sophist out of rhetoric, and the Socratist out of dialectic—Hegel felt that Socratism would always win as it had in ancient times, while Sophistry would always lose. We are not so sure about this now. Derrida is trying to present deconstruction as an ethic of discussion, based on the negative absolute of *différance*; Bakhtin has offered us the dialogical as an ethical principle; Habermas bases his ethic on communication; and even Rorty privileges the notion of conversation. We can take all these efforts, different—and even opposed—as they are, to be symptoms of this age's sophistical desire to make an ethic out of rhetoric. Can the trick be done? Let us keep that question open as we consider some possible relationships between rhetoric and ethics.

Rhetoric is a word that can be used to mean almost anything, a word that Humpty-Dumpty, no mean rhetorician himself, must have delighted in. Humpty-Dumpty, you will remember, said that words had to mean exactly what he intended them to mean. You will recall what happened to Humpty-Dumpty. At the risk of joining in this omelet, I shall begin by suggesting a definition for rhetoric. What I mean to investigate as rhetoric is the practice of reading, seen as an exchange for which textuality is the medium. Under the heading of rhetoric, we shall consider reading as a textual economy, in which pleasure and power are exchanged between producers and consumers of texts, always remembering that writers must consume in order to produce and that readers must produce in order to consume. On the other hand, under the heading of ethics, we shall be considering—and not apart from rhetoric but always intertwined with it—questions of the functions, effects, and ends of writing and reading. What is reading *for*? Can an ethic of reading serve as a guide in every ethical-political situation? That is, can all of life be described as a kind of reading, so that an ethic of reading will be an ethic for all of life? The view presented in these pages is that reading can indeed be an ethical activity but that reading does not incorporate all of ethics. To put the matter with perhaps excessive simplicity, reading a book is one thing, throwing it at someone is another. To be sure, the act of throwing can be read, but it is not itself only a reading. The world is a text, but it is not only a text. Some of these issues have been dramatized for us recently in the attempts by deconstructive critics to read feminism.

Deconstruction has been denounced by Jurgen Habermas as a mere critique of style, an attempt to give rhetoric an improper priority over logic—a charge to which Derrida has replied, "That is false, I say *false*, as opposed to *true*" (*Limited Inc*, 157). Derrida goes on to accuse Habermas of behaving unethically by making accusations without citing—and apparently without reading—Derrida's texts. I do not want to step between these heavyweight antagonists, but I suspect that Derrida is justified in his response. And yet. And yet, when he comes to discuss ethics on this and other occasions, what Derrida actually presents is a morality of reading rather than an assessment of action. It is true that he tries to extend the notions of reading and text as far as they will go, but I am not convinced that they go far enough. When Stanley Rosen charges contemporary philosophers with seeking to turn politics into hermeneutics, he may have a point. To borrow Derrida's own language, in the ethical-political realm deconstruction may be an indispensable guardrail but it will not necessarily get us anywhere. There is a fastidiousness about deconstruction that prevents it from fully engaging ethical-political issues. The extent to which deconstruction resists the ethical political is perhaps best revealed in the attempted deconstruction of feminism.

Feminism and deconstruction are both ways of reading—ways of making sense of the world. And both have sought to reach into the ethical-political world, as in Derrida's writings against apartheid and in many feminist projects to improve the condition of women. As methods of reading, however, they differ in significant ways. Deconstruction aspires to a certain universality and durability as a method. Feminism, on the other hand, is based upon the notion of a gendered reader, and it is driven by a perception of injustice in the relations between men and women in specific social, economic, and political terms. With respect to literary criticism, over the past decade or so feminists have forced upon a largely unwilling critical establishment many new and persuasive readings of classic texts and have brought about important changes in the literary canon. And in terms of literary theory, feminism has made a powerful contribution by framing the question of reading inside the question of gender. More than any other critical approach feminism has enabled us to see the folly of thinking about reading in terms as a transcendental process: the ideal reader reading a text that is the same for all. This does not happen.

Readers are constituted differently and different readers perceive different features of the same texts. Both texts and readers are already written when they meet, but both may emerge from the encounter altered in some crucial respect. Feminist critics have made this semiotic process concrete and intelligible for us all, for gender—if not destiny—is one of those rough spots by which necessity, in the form of culture, grasps us and shapes our ends. Because women in this culture have been an underprivileged class, they have learned lessons in class consciousness that many men have not. Because it cuts across social class, gender brings the lessons of class consciousness into places normally so insulated by privilege as to be unconscious of the structure that supports and insulates them. Feminism, then, has drawn its strength from the ethical-political domain, by showing that women, as a class, have been regularly discriminated against by a cultural system that positions them as subordinate to men.

The issue of class, therefore, has been important for feminist criticism as it has not been for deconstruction—and this is a major point upon which my treatment of these two critical modes will depend. For this reason it is important to clarify the notion of *class* that I will be using in this discussion. I do not mean to restrict the term to socioeconomic class, though that remains as a central type or model for the concept of *class* I am deploying here. Readers who read as members of a class can be distinguished from those who are members of what Stanley Fish has called an "interpretive community" (a concept with weaknesses I discussed in *Textual Power*), in that membership in a class implies both necessity and interest. A member of the class *Jew* in Hitler's Germany or of the class *Black* in South Africa at present is a member of those classes by necessity and has an interest in the situation of the class as a whole. And so, in those same societies, would a member of the class *Aryan* or *White* have such an interest. A class, in this sense, is a cultural creation, part of a system of categories imposed upon all those who attain subjectivity in a given culture. One may belong to a party or faction through choice—or what is perceived as choice—but one is assigned to a class by a system that allows no abstentions. One may choose to be a feminist or not, but one is assigned one's gender and may change it only by extraordinary effort. The relationship between being female and being a feminist is neither simple nor to be taken for granted, but there is no comparable relationship between being a deconstructionist and belonging to a class—which is of course not to say that deconstruction is free of interest or beyond ideology. Deconstructive critics constitute a party or faction within academic institutions and discourses. One joins this party only by actively professing the deconstructive faith and producing discourse that partakes of the deconstructive paradigm. The model here is quite clearly that of the sciences, even though the burden of deconstructive discourse is often antiscientific. Within academic institutions deconstructive critics, like those of other persuasions, seek power, status, and such other rewards as the institution may provide. But the deconstructive reader is in certain respects an ideal reader rather than a reader grounded in specific historical circumstances.

Within academic life feminism has come to be constituted in a manner similar to deconstruction, but with some absolutely crucial differences that turn precisely on this matter of class. Feminists claim a purpose and an authority that is based on their membership in a class extending beyond the bounds of academic institutions and their discourses. A feminist literary critic writes for other critics, to be sure, but she also writes on behalf of other women, and, as a critic, she is strengthened by the consciousness of this responsibility. A male critic, on the other hand, may work within the feminist paradigm but never be a full-fledged member of the class of feminists. On the same problems, the same texts, he will never work with the authority of a woman until the difference between male and female becomes insignificant. Feminism is especially interesting and especially valuable because of the way that class and paradigm come together under its banner. Feminism is not just a way of reading but a way of reading based upon ethical-political concerns.

The female reader proposed by feminism is not an individual reading for herself but a class-conscious member of the class *woman* reading on behalf of all the members of that class including herself. The power of feminist readings of texts depends to a great extent on the size and solidarity of this group and the clarity of the paradigm of reading that they share. Feminism has made its way against considerable open and tacit resistance from male critics—and some female critics—because individual members of the class *woman*, reading consciously as women, have produced highly similar readings of a variety of texts and found similar structures of patriarchy operating throughout the established canon and in the works of male interpreters of the canon. A shared critical paradigm driven by feminist class-consciousness has enabled these achievements.

The notion of *class* operative in feminism has a powerful social dimension, then, but there is also a linguistic/logical dimension to this notion, which is an indispensable part of the social functioning of the concept. In language most nouns denote categories or classes of objects, as the word *cat* denotes not this or that particular animal but a class of animals to which certain individuals can be assigned, and the word *woman* denotes a class of humans to which certain individuals can be assigned. In the history of Western thought, attitudes toward these class concepts or universals have shifted in a way that W. K. Wimsatt summarized usefully in an essay written four decades ago:

One main difference between all modern positivistic, nominalistic, and semantic systems and the scholastic and classical systems is that the older ones stress the similarity of the individuals denoted by the common term and hence the real universality of meaning, while the modern systems stress the differences in the individuals, the constant flux even of each individual in time and space and its kinetic structure, and hence infer only an approximate or nominal universality of meaning and a convenience rather than a truth in the use of general terms. [Wimsatt, 70]

Deconstruction, then, would be one of those modern systems that, as Wimsatt said, "stress the differences in the individuals." What

Wimsatt could not have predicted forty years ago was that a modern system would come along and reject "approximate or nominal universality" as if it were a fatal flaw in Western thought never noticed until now—indeed as if the Wittgensteinian concept of "family resemblance" had not been developed in response to a widespread awareness of the imperfection of universal categories. But deconstruction did come along and found itself upon the impurity of class concepts. Which means—in the present context—that we should be aware that feminism and deconstruction—and you can see it in the very names—are based on antithetical principles: feminism upon a class concept and deconstruction upon the deconstructing of all such concepts. This is why recent attempts—by Derrida himself and by Jonathan Culler—to incorporate feminism within deconstruction are so important for our consideration of the rhetoric and ethics of critical reading. We can begin by looking at Culler's reading of feminism in the section of his book *On Deconstruction* called "Reading as a Woman" and some other related passages from that book, seen against the background of Derrida's own deconstruction reading of feminism.

Culler seeks to appropriate feminism for deconstruction by reading the recent history of feminism in a particular way. He reads by writing. In this case what he writes is a story: a quest narrative in which feminism appears as the protagonist and deconstruction is positioned as the proper goal for this heroine's quest. The story, like many such tales, traces the heroine through three episodes, which Culler calls "moments" or "levels." This is the story of Feminism's Progress, which is similar to the progress of every pilgrim. For Culler, feminism's first moment finds the heroine at a level of naive belief in the feminine as a quality given by experience. In the second moment she has progressed to an awareness that the feminine must be generated by a struggle against the false consciousness imposed upon all readers by a patriarchal culture. The third moment is the present, and in it we find our heroine approaching the Holy City, which she may or may not be found worthy to enter. This pilgrimage has been a passage from a too earthy obsession with experience—with living as a woman—toward a nirvana in which all experience is transcended. In the perfection of the third stage—if our heroine can attain it—she will find "a larger textual system" (Culler, 61), and with this new instru-

ment she will obtain power over the categories of thought produced
by male authority: namely, "notions of realism, of rationality, of
mastery, of explanation" (62). This power will be manifested in the
heroine's ability to incorporate these notions within the activated
"larger textual system."

The larger textual system that can contain and thus have power over
realism, rationality, mastery, and *explanation* is, of course, deconstruction. There are, however, three serious problems in this positioning of
deconstruction as the final level of perfection to be achieved by feminism. First, as will be clear when we examine the concluding words of
the essay, and as Derrida himself has said quite bluntly, one of the
things deconstruction deconstructs is feminism itself. And second, to
position realism, rationality, mastery, and explanation as masculine is
to essentialize the male gender—a gesture supposedly abhorrent to
deconstruction. Finally, we should note that the reward for achieving
the third level is couched in terms of a "larger system"—a phrase that
clearly implicates *rationality, mastery,* and *explanation* in those two
words *larger* and *system.* Larger things master smaller ones of the same
order, and a large system must rationally explain more things than a
small system. Mastery is not abandoned here but reasserted, along
with rationality and explanation, as a quality of the "larger," deconstructive system.

Culler's inability to avoid concepts of *order* and *power* must lead the
critical reader to contemplate several possibilities. One such possibility is that deconstruction is as interested in order and power as any
other mode of discourse, and therefore just as thoroughly patriarchal.
If this is the case, deconstruction is not the proper goal for a feminism
that defines itself as opposed to order and power. The second possibility is that order and power are such pervasive features of thought
and discourse that there is simply no case for assigning them exclusively to one side of a binary system based on gender, nor is there
any way that deconstruction itself can avoid them. In this view, which
I personally accept, all textuality involves order and power. There is a
third possibility, of course, that perhaps Culler has just got it wrong,
that he has misrepresented deconstructive thought and his use of a
term like "larger system" is neither a conscious revelation nor an
unconscious one but a simple error. This may be the case, but I do not

believe it. I think that he has, if anything, overrepresented deconstruction, explaining its implications too clearly, thus bringing to light difficulties that less gifted or less ingenuous expositors repress. For example, as he considers feminism and deconstruction together, he identifies certain problems that defy solution, and he expresses reservations about Derrida's attempt to bring the two together in *Éperons*, which he calls "a relevant but unsatisfying document in this case" (61*n*). In this instance, it is precisely Culler's attempt to treat both feminism and deconstruction adequately that has led him to these "reservations" and perhaps to others, which sometimes take the form of narrative or assertive compensations for misgivings about the whole enterprise. One of the things that makes the conjunction of feminism and deconstruction interesting is that both positions have difficulty in determining their relationship to order and power. Culler's enactment of these difficulties seems to me exemplary.

The difficulties become especially apparent as the story of feminism's progress, and the text in which it is narrated, come to a conclusion. In this conclusion, as I read it, Culler suggests that one may seem to renounce that vile, male thing, authority, and yet have it after all by entering the pure, genderless discourse of deconstruction. Where this transcendence would leave those goals of feminism that are social and economic is one of the points that causes Culler and Derrida himself considerable difficulty. Culler takes it up again in his section on "Institutions and Inversions," directing our attention to Derrida's observation in *Positions* that the "phase of reversal" (Culler's translation, 165) or "phase of overturning" (Bass's translation, *Positions*, 41) hierarchical oppositions is necessary and must be gone through. Derrida is not talking specifically about the hierarchical opposition of *male* and *female* at this moment, but Culler quite properly inserts this citation as reflecting Derrida's views on the matter of gender relations. Culler also deftly cuts off the quotation at the point where Derrida takes back the word *phase* with its narrative or temporal thrust—and then reinstates temporality, and the word *phase* itself, in the next paragraph:

When I say that this phase is necessary, the word *phase* is perhaps not the most rigorous one. It is not a question of a chronological phase, a given moment, or a page that one day simply will be turned, in order to go on to other things. The necessity of this phase is structural; it is the necessity of interminable analysis: the hierarchy of dual oppositions always reestablishes itself. . . .

   That being said—and on the other hand—to remain in this phase is still to operate on the terrain of and from within the deconstructed system. [Derrida, *Positions*, 42]

   The concepts of temporality and progress are used, then apologized for and apparently abandoned, and finally reinstated powerfully with the words *remain, still,* and *phase* itself. Buried in the midst of this verbal cloud is the question of whether the hierarchy that reestablishes itself is the same as the one previously established (in our case male over female) or some different one, such as female over male. In other words, the question that needs asking here is whether the phase of reversal ever accomplishes anything in social terms. Does deconstructive practice assume that it can change the world? Or does it hold such goals to be naive and vulgar? I would say that this is not a rhetorical question, except that I fear an answer like "Both. And neither." Perhaps it is not so much a rhetorical question as a question of rhetoric. One of the large issues at stake in the conjunction of feminism and deconstruction is precisely the question of what the experience of being a woman has to do with one's ability to read as a woman. The relationship between experience and reading is absolutely crucial. Culler deals with it by deconstructing the notion of experience.

   In the third mode, the appeal to experience is veiled but still there, as a reference to maternal rather than paternal relations or to woman's situation and experience of marginality, which may give rise to an altered mode of reading. The appeal to the experience of the reader provides leverage for displacing or undoing the system of concepts or procedures of male criticism, but "experience" always has this divided, duplicitous character: it has always already occurred and yet is still to be produced—an indispensable point of reference, yet never simply there. [Culler, 63]

"Experience" here, neatly veiled with quotation marks by the end of the passage, has a curiously vague and diffuse quality. When one achieves the third level of feminism one may refer airily to "maternal relations" or the marginality of "woman" in general, but not to anything so vulgar as the experience of living in a female body as opposed to a male one. "Experience," in this discourse, is something to be alluded to rather than something one lives through or, as we say, experiences.

I agree that a person may have experiences but, lacking the proper discursive codes, not be conscious of them or of their import. I only want to insist that there is a difference between having an experience and not having it, and a very large and significant difference between having the same experience over and over again and never having that experience at all. Deconstruction, I am afraid, must deny that very difference, for the following reasons. The fundamental gesture in the edifice of deconstructive thought is the denial of any significant difference between speech and writing, on the grounds that the apparent distinction between the copresence of speaker and listener in speech and their mutual absence in writing is not a real distinction, there being no such thing as pure presence. The same line of thought, if accepted, must lead us to the conclusion that there is no significant difference between reading about an experience and having an experience, because experience never simply occurs. As Culler puts it, experience "has always already occurred yet is still to be produced."

Very revealingly, Derrida's way of dealing with the question of feminine experience is to turn it into a question of essence, which he can then subject to the deconstructive formula, demonstrating that there is no such thing as a purely, essentially feminine creature:

Now, when you say that "it's getting to be a watch word that in your writings the feminine can only be read as a metaphor," then I would say "no." . . . It's not a metaphor. It's not a metaphor first off because in order for the feminine to be a metaphor one would have to be assured of knowing what the *essence propre* of woman is. . . . And what I try to say particularly in *Spurs* (*Éperons*) is that woman has no essence of her very own, and that that's the phallocentric gesture. It's the gesture of considering that there is "*la femme*" and that she has her very own essence. ["Deconstruction in America: An Interview with Jacques Derrida," 31]

We should perhaps note in passing that a very strange notion of metaphor is invoked here, according to which no word can be metaphorical unless the essence of its referent is perfectly known. By this logic, since we can never know the essence of anything perfectly, nothing is metaphorical—or everything is, and all the cows start turning black again before our eyes. We should also note, however, that by collapsing the problem of feminine experience into the question of feminine essence, Derrida achieves mastery over feminism. He insists that feminism is in fact a form of phallogocentrism:

For me deconstruction is certainly not feminist. At least as I have tried to practice it, I believe it naturally supposes a radical deconstruction of phallogocentrism, and certainly an absolutely other and new interest in women's questions. But if there is one thing that it must not come to, it's feminism. So I would say that deconstruction is a deconstruction of feminism, from the start, insofar as feminism is a form—no doubt necessary at a certain moment—but a form of phallogocentrism among many others. ["Interview," 30]

It is precisely the attempt of women to use their own experience as authority for reading or writing in a certain way that Derrida rejects or accepts as an evil necessary only for a certain "moment." It is as though phallogocentric feminism will do the dirty work so that androgynous deconstruction can then enjoy the fruits of this labor—except that what deconstruction really enjoys is deconstructing feminism even while it is struggling to achieve its political and economic goals—goals that depend to some extent upon the ability of women to be conscious of themselves as a class—however impure—bound by a certain shared experience. The question of feminine experience is taken up several times in Culler's text, and always on those occasions we find difficulties at the surface of the text that are symptomatic of deeper conceptual problems. One such point is the final paragraph of "Reading as a Woman," in which Culler rewrites Peggy Kamuf's description of *writing* as a woman in the form of a statement about *reading* as a woman, drawing the following conclusion:

For a woman to read as a woman is not to repeat an identity or an experience that is given but to play a role she constructs with reference to her identity as a woman, which is also a construct, so the series can continue: a woman reading as a woman reading as a woman. The non-

coincidence reveals an interval, a division within woman or within any
reading subject and the "experience" of that subject. [Culler, 64]

From the heights of deconstruction we are given a glimpse into the
bottomless abyss of textuality, a vertiginous perspective in which
constructs are erected upon constructs, without foundation and without end. Such a world seems to offer a dazzling textual freedom, but
in practice deconstructive discourse rarely displays the liberated grace
that one might expect to find in it; instead it seems constrained by
fears of falling into locutions of presence and thus becoming prey for
the monster Phallogocentrism. In the present instance Culler's own
discourse falters even as he describes the textual abyss, becoming
ungrammatical, unclear, and phallogocentric all at once.

The phallogocentrism appears in the first clause, which makes a
powerful truth claim: "For a woman to read as a woman is not
to . . . but to . . . " In this expression one can find *realism, rationality,
mastery,* and *explanation:* all those things that Culler has previously
assigned to "male authority" and phallogocentric discourse. Culler is
explaining to us here what *really* happens when a woman reads as a
woman. not *that,* but *this.* He *reasons* effectively in this way because
the "larger system" of deconstruction has given him *mastery* over such
matters as reading and writing. This combination of textual order and
power is in fact entirely typical of academic and many other forms of
discourse. It would not be worth noting if Culler had not assigned it
to the phallogocentric monster in the first place. Even so, it is probably the least interesting problem in the passage we are considering.

The logical problems appear next. They appear largely in the following section of the first sentence in the passage: "not to repeat an
identity or an experience that is given but to play a role she constructs
with reference to her identity as a woman, which is also a construct."
This is binary thinking with a vengeance. We are offered two versions
of what it might be to function as a woman. One version is *repeating a
given identity.* The other is *playing a role that one constructs.* The first is
boring, mechanical, totally deterministic. The second is fun, creative,
and free. Not hard to choose between these two possibilities! But
what has this stark choice got to do with the experience of living as a

woman? Surely the first alternative exaggerates the determinism involved in functioning as a member of any class whatsoever. And just as
surely the second alternative exaggerates the freedom available to any
individual, whether reading a text or performing any other human
activity. There is, of course, a qualifying clause in the second alternative. One is to play one's role "with reference to" one's identity as a
member of the class in question—an "identity" which is itself already
a kind of role, a "construct"—but constructed by whom we do not
know. What, I wonder, can "with reference to" mean in this context?
Does it mean that one is absolutely free to accept, reject, or modify
this identity? If so, in what sense can it be the identity *of* the person
concerned? For that matter, why call it an "identity" if it is not identi-
cal to itself. Identity is what persists. If nothing persists, then no
identity is in question. Why, in any case, must we think of "her"
identity as female? That is, to what extent is it necessary to speak of
this constructed identity using the feminine pronoun *her*. Could *she*
read with reference to her identity as a man, which would certainly be
a construct? Could we even speak of "her identity as a man"? If we
could not, then gender must be something more than a role that we
can accept or reject with entire freedom. Surely this is a case where
rigorous thought ought to see gender as both a given and a construct.
My point is that the deconstructive terminology does not clarify—as
deconstructive discourse does at its best—but obscures a complex
situation, leaving the real problems of freedom and determination
with respect to gender inadequately discussed.

There are similar and perhaps even more important problems with
the concept of experience in this passage. In the first part of the
statement that we are trying to read, identity and experience are
presented as equivalents: "not to repeat an *identity* or *experience* that is
given." In the second part, experience is dropped and only identity is
mentioned: "with reference to her *identity* as a woman, which is also a
construct." Assuming that this dropping of *experience* is significant, let
us reinstate it in place of *identity* and see what happens. With such a
change, the crucial phrase will read "her *experience* as a woman, which
is also a construct." Is experience a construct? If so, it is not just a
construct but something that constructs. That is, a woman's experi-

ences are things that have happened to her and are still happening to her, even as she writes. She does not step outside of them to refer to them from some transcendental perspective. To the extent that she is able to refer to them, to distance them by giving them verbal expression, we may say she is outside them, but she can never get completely outside them, and it is the recognition of this that constitutes her conscious membership in the class of women. This woman is what she is because she has had one set of experiences rather than another, some of which typified the experiences of other members of the class of women at a particular point in history. The introduction and later suppression of the term *experience* is a symptom of the text's inability to deal with this concept within the framework of deconstructive thought.

Derrida is troubled by the same problems, which he addresses in a light and impromptu manner at the end of the interview from which I have quoted.

In other words if we consider for example what is called a writing man— for example me, to the extent that I'm supposed to be a man—then writing on woman should be less writing on woman than writing from or on the basis of [*depuis*] what comes to me from a feminine place. ["Interview," 32]

Following Culler, we can rewrite this as a comment on reading:

If we consider for example what is called a reading man—for example me, to the extent that I'm supposed to be a man—then reading as a woman should be less reading as a woman than reading from or on the basis of what comes to me from a feminine place.

Yes, possibly, but where is this "feminine place" and on what basis does a man have access to it? In deconstructive terms it is the trace of femininity that is inevitably inscribed in something defined as *not* feminine. But to reason in this way is to give the trace a positive status as a place or locus of the feminine. The "feminine place" here is perhaps not strictly deconstructive but Jungian. Still, one must wonder exactly what does come from this feminine place and how it might be recognized or authenticated as feminine. Derrida's awareness of the problem is suggested by his immediate restatement of it in terms of voice: "I too have learned from the *écoute* of women, from listening to the degree I can to a certain feminine voice." Of special interest here is the qualification: "to the degree I can." What is it, we must ask, that sets limits to Derrida's ability to hear "a certain feminine voice"? Why does he need to suggest that he hears this voice less well than he hears other (presumably masculine) voices? What can it be other than his own membership in the class of males, with all that implies in the way of experience? At some level the concept of *experience*, which was earlier dismissed and replaced by the more docile and vulnerable concept of *essence*, is returning to trouble this text also.

Quite properly Derrida wants to complicate the question of gender, to deconstruct it,

Because it's not such a simple thing when we say that whoever bears a masculine proper name, is anatomically male, etc., is a man. This feminine voice can pass through trajectories that are extremely multiple. . . . In other words, on the other side, and even in the most feminist women, the masculine voice is not silent. ["Interview," 32]

Still, after these words the text indicates "LAUGHTER." This laughter I read as symptomatic. Feminism and feminists have, however gently and gracefully, been put in their place—again. Whenever women speak up, it is the phallogocentric male voice speaking through them. And when they read actively and aggressively as members of the class *woman*, are they then reading through male eyes as well? Or are they finally reading as women conscious of their own experience as members of a class who share that experience?

Feminism, as I have been suggesting, approaches the question of an ethics of reading from a social and historical standpoint that is connected to an ideal of justice. The feminist reader is a woman reading on behalf of the class of women—or a man trying to assume that role. Deconstruction, on the other hand, tries to deal with the question of an ethics of reading from an immanent perspective, with reading generating its own ethic of freeplay or rigorous exorbitance. This ethic secretly draws its strength, however, from either an ideal of Nietzschean playfulness or a more Hegelian ideal of rational freedom—or perhaps from the impossible merger of these two. The deconstructive reader, as I have suggested, reads as a member of an interpretive community, while the feminist reader reads as a member of a class. Furthermore, deconstruction, as Derrida's Afterword to *Limited Inc* makes clear, is more concerned with an ethics of reading than with a reading of ethics. Deconstruction, as we shall see again at the end of this chapter, resists the notion that there is a significant difference between reading and action. To act, as Derrida pointed out with respect to feminism, is to implicate oneself in that which one is acting against. To struggle against patriarchal practices in the social arena is to become contaminated with patriarchal attitudes. There is, in deconstruction, a certain reluctance to stop reading and throw the book at somebody, a reluctance to stop the play of textuality and accept the limitations of action. I am reminded, in this connection, of something Hegel said in lecturing on the logical part of his *Encyclo-paedia*: "People who are too fastidious towards the finite never reach actuality, but linger lost in abstraction, and their light dwindles away" (Hegel, sec. 92).

Deconstruction and feminism, in the confrontation I have described, function in somewhat—but only somewhat—the same way as the Sophist and Socratist described by Hegel in the epigraph to this chapter (*Logic*, par. 121, addition). The Sophist detaches evaluation from absolutes and makes it a matter of the technique of persuasion, of rhetoric. The Socratist, on the other hand, seeks to connect evaluation to the absolutes of justice and will, with texts as well as actions being evaluated ethically. I have suggested that feminism bases itself on an absolute of justice, whereas deconstruction acknowledges only the negative absolute of affirmation or play, though it covertly (through terms like *rigor*) has recourse to a more positive absolute of rationality. I have also argued that feminism accepts the limitations of social and political action, while deconstruction, to preserve its freedom, avoids the limitations of commitment. Thus feminism acknowledges an extratextual ethic while deconstruction does not. We shall return to the question of deconstruction and ethics at the end of this chapter, but first we must look further into the workings of rhetoric. We shall begin this part of our investigation by positioning rhetoric not against ethics but against poetics.

Much of our formal study of the rhetoric of reading has been

grounded, consciously or not, upon a notion of rhetoric that is sometimes thought to have an ancient pedigree but is actually the product
of Romantic thinkers. We are especially familiar with it because it was
restated powerfully by the major figures of modernist literature in the
early part of this century. It is deeply embedded, for instance, in the
thinking of both William Butler Yeats and James Joyce. In this view
rhetoric is located in binary opposition to something called poetry,
literature, or art, with rhetoric occupying the negative slot in this
highly charged binarism. Joyce, for instance, tells us that proper art
leads to contemplation of the aesthetic object, while improper art (or
rhetoric) moves us to action rather than contemplation. Yeats says, in
a beautifully telling phrase, that he makes rhetoric out of his quarrels
with others and poetry out of his quarrels with himself. Such a view
positions rhetoric as a study of improper art, the theory and practice
of manipulative textuality, as opposed to the pure textuality of art or
literature. This view would seem to make rhetoric the perfect way of
approaching advertising, for instance, which is widely held to be the
improperest and impurest form of text known to humanity, but a
quite improper way to approach poetry, which is by definition free
from the taint of rhetoric. In the pages that follow, I shall be arguing
against this view. It is an open question, I believe, whether, as Derrida
might have put it, there is any form of textuality outside of rhetoric.
And even if we allow that there may be some sort of logic or dialectic
that transcends the rhetoric of textuality, neither literature nor propaganda can be seen as transcendental. Much of my effort, then, in the
following discussion, will be devoted to undoing the accepted distinction between poetry and advertising.

We should begin, perhaps, by noting that this opposition between
rhetoric and aesthetics was developed and deployed by post-En-
lightenment thinkers. A. G. Baumgarten is usually credited with in-
troducing the term *aesthetics* (in the sense of the study of "taste") to
European discourse in the middle of the eighteenth century. In English the word appears—and is contested—only in the 1830s. The
noun *aesthete*, it is worth noting, does not occur in English for another
half century, appearing just in time for James Joyce's birth. The concept of aesthetic activity is connected, historically and logically, with

the notion of art and literature as an autonomous area of human life that might be studied under the heading of taste or judgment. In contrast to this, we should remember that Plato and Aristotle position rhetoric in binary opposition not to poetry but to dialectic, the arts of persuasion being opposed to the search for truth. Plato, of course, sees poetry in opposition to dialectic, as well. For him poetry and rhetoric share a deplorable lack of concern for truth. For Plato, these oppositions are normally quite invidious: dialectic is good; rhetoric and poetry are bad—or at least highly suspect. Aristotle is much less absolute. In his view, rhetoric and dialectic are "counterparts" (see the opening of the *Rhetoric*) that function together in human discourse, meeting in the form of the enthymeme. He also suggests that rhetoric and poetry are closely allied, both being designed to arouse the passions and thus necessarily using many of the same means to accomplish these same ends.

The point of this brief excursion into the history of rhetorical and aesthetic theory is to suggest that a rhetoric of reading will do better to take its departure from Aristotle than from the modernist heirs of Romanticism. I say Aristotle and not Plato, here, for reasons that I trust will be obvious. Plato prefers and seeks purity of form. His dialectic is in fact a method for the purification of thought. Aristotle, on the other hand, is comfortable among the mixed forms of ordinary living. In particular, he tells us early in his treatise on the subject that rhetoric "has to do with things about which we commonly deliberate—things for which we have no special art or science; and with the sort of hearers who cannot grasp many points in a single view, or follow a long chain of reasoning" (para. 1357a). All but a few of our contemporary texts may be said to exist in this mode of textuality. That is, most of what we read and write does not come in the form of long chains of reasoning. Indeed, I will, in a properly postmodern manner, go beyond Aristotle and assert that no text is ever purely reasonable, just as I have gone beyond or against the Romantics in asserting that no text is ever purely aesthetic. We are all inside rhetoric. It is the textual medium in which we live.

This is not the occasion, nor am I the person, to offer anything approaching a full Aristotelian analysis of the aims and devices of modern rhetoric. It should be possible, however, to consider a few representative texts in the light of Aristotelian principles and in the spirit of Aristotelian investigation. Aristotle, you will remember, recognized three types of persuasion: that based on the character of the speaker, that based on controlling the emotion of th audience, and that based upon reasoning or argument. Perhaps I should make it clear that I have no desire to deny the possibilities of reason. After all, I am trying to be reasonable—or to give the appearance of being reasonable—myself. What I am asserting, however, is that reason always comes to us textualized with emotion. What a text *is* can be described as a texture, a textile, woven of threads of reason and threads of emotion. It is precisely this texture that I will try to discuss here in terms of a metaphor of textual economy—that is to say, in terms of some exchange of values for which texts are the medium.

Textual economy is marked, in particular, by exchanges of power and pleasure. The rhetoric of textual economy that I am proposing, then, will take the form of an investigation into the flow of pleasure and power that is organized by any text. Both texts and other forms of human intercourse may be described as systems in which power and pleasure are exchanged. For instance, there is a profound analogy between textual and sexual exchanges—an analogy of which T. S. Eliot, for instance (to name a modernist with a more developed notion of rhetoric than that of Yeats or Joyce) was fully aware. Eliot put textual matters in terms of an eroto-political metaphor that may help us get our bearings here. In a letter he wrote to Stephen Spender in 1935, Eliot described our reading of literary texts in the following words: "You don't really criticize any author to whom you have never surrendered yourself. . . . Even just the bewildering minute counts; you have to give yourself up, and then recover yourself, and the third moment is having something to say, before you have wholly forgotten both surrender and recovery." Frank Kermode, whose discussion of this passage provides the point of departure for me here (Eliot, 13) notes that the expression "bewildering minute," which Eliot had used in two of his important essays in addition to this letter to Spender, is taken from a passage in a Jacobean play by Tourneur or Middleton, in which the question is asked, "Are lordships sold to maintain ladyships / For the poor benefit of a bewildering minute?"

As Kermode points out, in their context the lines refer quite unambiguously to the erotic experience of "sexual surrender," and he perspicuously traces Eliot's transformation of them in *The Waste Land* ("blood shaking my heart / The awful daring of a moment's surrender") as well as in other poems and essays, where they are used to signify both sexual and spiritual surrenders. What Eliot and Kermode both seem to overlook or suppress—in what we can now see as a typically modernist critical gesture—is the word *sold* in the original Jacobean quotation. The "bewildering minute" of pleasure is positioned by the playwright within a politicoeconomic system in which lordships may be exchanged for sexual pleasure. My rhetorical point here is simply that textual pleasure also always involves some surrender of sovereignty—and that this is true whether the text is a poem or an advertisement. *The Waste Land* itself is designed to persuade us of the degradation (or abjection, as Calvin Bedient would have it) of a life without religious commitment, and we cannot "surrender" to the pleasure of Eliot's text without at least trying on his beliefs during that bewildering moment of surrender. *The Waste Land,* then, is rhetorical in just the sense that I am proposing for that term. What it does, in its own way and for its own audience, is exactly what all texts that offer us pleasure—including advertising commercials—do for their audiences. The differences are only in the constraints and opportunities offered by the different media. The economy of power and pleasure is the same. And these textual exchanges all begin with the bewildering minute.

Since my approach by way of Eliot may seem excessively tainted with the ideology of high modernism (not to mention high Anglicanism), it will be well to mention how nicely this view of textual rhetoric accords with the perspective developed by the now largely forgotten behavioristic semiotician Charles Morris. In his brilliant but cranky book, *Signs, Language, and Behavior,* Morris described poetry as "discourse which is primarily appraisive-valuative." Whitman was his prime example of the poetic use of appraisive signs, his chief illustration being the following passage from "Song of Myself":

I believe in the flesh and the appetites,
Seeing, hearing, feeling are miracles, and each part and tag of me is a
miracle.

Divine am I inside and out, and I make holy whatever I touch or am
   touched from.
The scent of these arm-pits aroma finer than prayer,
This head more than churches, bibles, and all the creeds.

[Morris, 136]

When I first read Morris twenty years ago I thought that he was
having serious difficulty distinguishing poetry from advertising and
propaganda. I still think so, but now I am convinced that this difficulty was actually the sign of an important notion trying to emerge in
Morris's thought—even though he resisted it fiercely—the notion
that poetry, advertising, and propaganda are not different in kind or
in method but are always intermingled, drawing their strength from
this very mixture more often than not. What Whitman is doing in the
quoted passage is working the analogical possibilities that connect the
human body to the body of religious beliefs—an analogy, be it said,
that had already received plenty of attention from within Christian
thought itself. Put bluntly, Whitman goes to a source of spiritual
value—and a source that specifically generates this value by opposing
it to carnality—and attempts to reverse the flow of value, to change
the polarity of the analogy. The most striking line in the quotation—
"The scent of these arm-pits aroma finer than prayer"—is itself based
on many biblical and other texts in which prayers ascend to the Lord
in just the way that the odor of sacrificial offerings is said to ascend.
One might even suppose that the missing mediating term between
Whitman's armpits and prayer is the incense that has been associated
with Christianity ever since the gifts of the Magi to Mary's babe.
Though not an Anglican Catholic, Whitman's metaphorical armpits
may be high in more than one sense.

   To make such an analysis is, among other things, to resist the power
of Whitman's text over us, to move from that moment of pleasurable
bewilderment in which we first encounter this singing of the body, in
which we yield to the power of Whitman's text, to a moment of
contemplation that is earned by our own analytic labor, the exertion
of our own power, which, of course, carries its own pleasure with it as
well. The rhetorical exchange is never a simple binary trade, as we shall
see in more than one example. Before leaving Whitman and Charles

Morris, however, we should hear Morris more fully on the subject of
poetic language, and I will ask my readers to hear him in a double way,
imagining that his words apply to advertising as well as poetry:

> The great significance of poetic discourse [think also of advertising
> discourse] lies in the vivid and direct way that it records and sustains
> achieved valuations, and explores and strengthens novel valuations. In
> poetry the object signified is turned, as it were, before our eyes with
> symbolic fingers, and as we look at the object described and exemplified by
> the poet, we come in varying degrees and for a longer or shorter time to
> take the valuative perspective of the poet in terms of which the object
> signified has the apprehended significance. . . . Poetry then not merely
> records what men have found significant, but plays a dynamic role in the
> development and integration of valuative attitudes and explicit evaluations.
> [Morris, 138]

And so, of course, do propaganda and advertising attempt to play the
same sort of role in the "development and integration of valuative
attitudes." Though his own language is marred for us by its pseudo-
scientific behaviorism, Morris achieves a certain amount of eloquence
as his prose rises to the metaphor of poetry turning an object "before
our eyes with symbolic fingers" as a way of persuading us to share the
poet's evaluative perspective. In this moment of eloquence, Morris
becomes a poet or advertiser himself, offering us the pleasure of his
metaphor in order to gain our acceptance of his view of the object.
That is, he does what he says poetry does, only poetry itself is the
object that is "turned . . . before our eyes." Morris means to be "scientific" in his own discourse, but his most precise, delicate, and convincing moments are often those in which he is most rhetorical, as in
this case, where he uses "appraisive-valuative discourse" to convince
us that poetry is, in fact, "appraisive-valuative discourse."

Whitman, who after all worked for the *Brooklyn Eagle* once upon a
time, may seem an unfair choice to illustrate the advertising component of poetry—too much of the ad man in him from the beginning—
but I will maintain that there is scarcely a poem to be found that is not
characterized by what Morris called "appraisive-valuative discourse"
and by what I am calling exchanges of textual power and pleasure.
When Archibald MacLeish said "A poem should not mean / But be,"

he was concluding a poem (called "Ars Poetica") which can be read—
must be read—as a sales pitch for a certain imagist or modernist
product, a product which he tries, in the opening lines of the poem, to
push in the classic advertising manner, by associating it with objects
already appraised or valued highly:

A poem should be palpable and mute
As a globed fruit,

Dumb
As old medallions to the thumb,

Silent as the sleeve-worn stone
Of casement ledges where the moss has grown—

A poem should be wordless
As the flight of birds

[Sanders et al., II:308]

One may argue that MacLeish is no poet—at least upon this occasion—and that his "poem" is not "poetry"—but if this is so, most of
what has been called poetry will have to be thrown out along with
Whitman and MacLeish. William Carlos Williams, for instance, betrays himself when he begins one of his most famous poems with the
phrase "so much depends / upon / a red wheel / barrow." Which of us
can avoid desiring this textualized barrow, upon which so much depends? And how can we avoid seeing Williams as pushing this barrow? I have heard it said that the first two lines of this poem should
have been omitted, but I think the resulting haiku would still be
charged with evaluative meaning. Williams at his best, and his best is
quite wonderful, is often as happily appraisive as Whitman:

If I admire my arms, my face,
my shoulders, flanks, buttocks
against the yellow drawn shades,—

Who shall say I am not
the happy genius of my household?

[from "Danse Russe," in Sanders et al., II:153]

And who could resist having their charms presented in this way:

Your thighs are appletrees
whose blossoms touch the sky.

> [from "Portrait of a Lady," in Sanders et al., II:153]

One may say, of course, "Well, Williams, yes, a celebrator, a son of Walt, but hardly typical of all poets." Perhaps. Let us look at some others. Here are the last lines of a sonnet by Edna St. Vincent Millay:

It well may be that in a difficult hour,
Pinned down by pain and moaning for release,
Or nagged by want past resolution's power,
I might be driven to sell your love for peace.
  Or trade the memory of this night for food.
  It well may be. I do not think I would.

> [Sonnet 30, from *Fatal Interview*, in Sanders et al., II:303]

Evaluation could hardly be put into a more economically motivated language. The speaker of these lines would neither "sell" nor "trade" her love or her memories. The poem exists to express the value of these treasures, and the expression is enhanced in this case by the apparent refusal of hyperbole—as in Shakespeare's "My mistress' eyes are nothing like the sun." Like painters, poets who represent their objects with power and precision cannot help but make them take on a special interest. It is hard to look at a Monet, for instance—any Monet—without wanting to enter that painted world and live in it, breathing, eating, and drinking paint. It is hard to gaze upon the quiet world of Vermeer without coming to value excessively every object represented lovingly on those flat surfaces. In a similar way a bird described by Emily Dickinson becomes a precious bird, a desirable bird:

He glanced with rapid eyes
That hurried all around—
They looked like frightened Beads, I thought—
He stirred his Velvet Head

Like one in danger, Cautious,
I offered him a Crumb
And he unrolled his feathers
And rowed him softer home—

Than Oars divide the Ocean,
Too silver for a seam—
Or Butterflies, off Banks of Noon
Leap, plashless as they swim.
                    [from "A bird came down the Walk," in Sanders et al., II:16–17]

This, of course, is soft sell, and what is being sold, among other
things, is softness. Dickinson, however, also shows us her bird biting
a worm in two and eating, as she says "the fellow, raw," but that is in
the earlier part of the poem, where it functions like the *concessio* in an
argument, to bolster the ethos of the speaker and make the main point
more believable. This is both a real bird and a beautiful bird—beautiful in its entire birdness and not merely as a velvet-headed creature
who flies more softly than butterflies. We may say, I think, that
Dickinson's circumspection—present even in many of her shortest
poems—makes her appraisive vision especially powerful and pleasurable. In her understated way she could sell you a seat in heaven—or
"Eden," as she calls it—without half trying:

Maybe—"Eden" a'nt so lonesome
As New England used to be!
                    [from "What is—'Paradise,'" in Sanders et al., II:14]

   Most advertising rhetoric appraises things favorably, of course, but
that is because advertisers talk mainly about their own products. The
rhetoric of politics and propaganda, however, is extremely effective at
negative evaluation. So is some poetry. When Adrienne Rich quietly
observes (in "Amnesia") that "Becoming a man means leaving / someone, or something" she is offering us an interpretation of the snow
scene in *Citizen Kane*, as she indicates, but she is also describing, and
by describing it indicting, a whole cultural practice that constructs
manhood in terms of moving on, lighting out for the territory: a
practice that also constructs the female as what is left behind, what is
stationary, what needs to be abandoned for the male to become himself. Her evaluation is presented through the analogy between someone and something, between the mother left behind, for instance, in

that major American film, and the sled, Rosebud, left out in the snow.
"Why," she asks,

must the snow-scene blot itself out
the flakes come down so fast
so heavy, so unrevealing

over the something that gets left behind?

[Rich, 229–30]

The question is, as we say, rhetorical, asking us to perceive critically
not just this or that person's behavior, but a whole cultural practice.
This is a poem, to be sure, but it is also an interpretive essay and a
cultural critique. To accept the pleasure of that lucid, thoughtful
discourse is also to accept its feminist perspective, for at least the
bewildering moment. But poetry, like advertising, is more likely to
celebrate than to criticize. Joy is the force that drives much of our best
poetry, as Coleridge noted when he struggled so painfully to make a
poem out of his own dejection. Before turning to look at some
avowed advertising discourse, let us consider briefly one more passage
from a poem. Here is Mary Oliver, on a boat off Cape Cod, waiting
for a glimpse of some humpback whales:

We wait, not knowing
just where it will happen; suddenly
they smash through the surface, someone begins
shouting for joy and you realize
it is yourself as they surge
upward and you see for the first time
how huge they are, as they breach,
and dive, and breach again
through the shining blue flowers
of the split water and you see them
for some unbelievable
part of a moment against the sky—
like nothing you've ever imagined—
like the myth of the fifth morning galloping
out of darkness, pouring
heavenward, spinning; then

they crash back under those black silks
and we all fall back
together into that wet fire, you
know what I mean

[from "Humpbacks," in Oliver, 60–62]

And we do know—after Mary Oliver has told us. Would you buy a
used whale from Mary Oliver? Or a bird from Emily Dickinson? I
would. I couldn't resist. Of course, there is always the danger that the
actual thing would never achieve the beauty it has on the page—a
phenomenon I learned early from the *F. A. O. Schwartz Catalogue*—
but that is why some of us are poets or makers of catalogues, while
others are consumers of poems and catalogues to use as fuel for our
thoughts and dreams. The great trick, of course, would be to learn
from Emily Dickinson how to "see" a bird, so that our birds might be
more like hers. Poetry exists, as Viktor Shklovsky might have told us,
to make the bird birdy and the whale whaley, or even, as in the case of
Archibald MacLeish, to make the poem poemy. But of course one
makes the whale whaley by turning it into black silk in water that is
first blue flowers and then wet fire, as one makes the bird birdy by
constructing it out of velvet with a bead for an eye, flying through an
ocean of air, and one makes the poem poemy by asserting its necessary
resemblance to globed fruit, old medallions, sleeve-worn stone, and
the flight of birds. In just this way does advertising frequently sell its
wares, as Leo Spitzer pointed out four decades ago in his pioneering
essay on a Sunkist orange juice advertisement. Or, as a more recent
semiotic critic like Umberto Eco might put it, poems and ads exploit
the same metaphoric and metonymic pathways within the network of
unlimited semiosis to achieve their similar ends. What, then, if anything, is left as the difference between poetry and advertising? Before
attempting to answer this question, let us add to our set of examples
some overtly commercial texts.

Magazine advertising, of course, privileges the visual over the verbal, but even the most powerful images, as we shall see, derive their
rhetorical force from metaphoric and metonymic linkages. That is,
whether the signs are visual or verbal matters less in this rhetorical

economy than the fact that they are signs used in an appraisive-valu-ative system. We can find this textual economy at work, for instance, in an ad for "Savvy" fashion jewelry that appeared in a recent issue of *Vanity Fair*. The name "Savvy" appears to be derived from the manu-facturer's name—Swarovski—by a simple anagrammatic method that effectively turns a potential Polish joke into a lure for the woman who wants to be perceived as "knowing," "with it," or, in a word, "savvy." The verbal text of the ad appears at the bottom of the page, against a background of black, possibly velvet. It says, "Knowing who to lend an ear to is the mark of a **Savvy** woman." The phrase "lend an ear" comes, though at some remove, from the mouth of Shake-speare's master of rhetoric, Mark Antony. The visual image, however, revives this tired trope by taking it more literally than is usually the case. Above the black velvet we see part of the face of what appears to be a woman: an eye, part of an eyebrow, and an ear, connected by soft smooth skin, which we see so clearly that we can discern the almost invisible blond facial hair near the ear, coding the face as female. Attached to the earlobe is a large glittering jewel of an earring, pre-sumably made by Swarovski. This bejeweled ear is being lent, appar-ently, to a male, part of whose face is also visible inside our picture frame. We see him slightly from the rear: a bit of chin, the curve of a cheek, most of a nose, pressing up against the woman's face at a point midway between eyebrow and top of the ear, a little brown hair at this man's temple, and just enough hint of an incipient beard to signal to us that this is indeed a male face. He may be whispering into the ear of the woman, whose head is at a reclining angle, but he appears to be almost eating the top of her ear, which ends abruptly where his mouth obscures our view of it.

The woman's eyeball has rolled all the way toward where the man is. She seems to be lending him an eye as well. A bit of her own brown hair extends from behind the man's face out above her ear and then curves away, where her facial hair, very light and delicate, begins. The most striking thing about the entire image is the way in which the man's most prominent part—his projecting, convex nose—and the woman's most prominently positioned part—her intricately whorled concave ear—combine to make an unmistakably sexual conjunction:

a conjunction, be it said, in which the jewel made by Savvy falls into place in precisely the spot which in late ancient Greek could be called a jewel. This Savvy woman has lent her ear first to the firm of Swarovski America Limited and then to the male who is nibbling at it or whispering in it, with his nose probing her temple, but an ear is not always, or only, an ear. In the metaphor of lending, the erotic and the economic blend nicely. We do not know whether the jewel has been exchanged for the ear, but we are certainly alerted to some sort of transaction taking place before our eyes. The woman has the jewel because she is "savvy"—or is she savvy, as the ad suggests, because she has the jewel. Poems and ads often like to blur the line between mere contiguity and matters of cause-and-effect. At any rate, the Savvy woman, presumably, doesn't lend her ear, or any other part of her anatomy, to just anybody—nor is lending to be confused with giving. The jewel in the ad, as we have noticed, has been positioned artfully for maximum effect.

Advertising frequently goes for the sexual jugular. So, of course, do religion and poetry. Let us recall, for instance, John Donne's comparison between arrival at his beloved's nether parts and the discovery of America—not to mention what are now Canada's Maritime Provinces—("O my America! my new-found-land"). Advertising, like poetry, is also highly intertextual. We have seen how even Savvy is not above brushing up our Shakespeare. In the case of Georges Marciano, however, the author in the background, somewhat more subtly invoked, is Ernest Hemingway. I am referring to an ad which, in its original context, was part of a ten-page spread in *Vanity Fair* magazine, February 1988, advertising Guess Jeans. Although these images do not tell a complete story, they make a sequence based on a single theme. In one of these ten pages, the visual text is dominated by the image of an attractive young woman, posed against a background of wall posters, holding just above her forehead a pair of horns like those of a cow or bull. The photograph is in black and white, with only the name of the advertiser, Georges Marciano, scrawled across the page in bright red. We cannot miss the name, but its color separates it from the other images. The name is on the picture, not in it, like the signature of an artist on a painting, only much more prominent: as if it were written in red lipstick. The wall posters in the background are just clear enough for us to make out what they are about.

Since these ten pages of advertising are not directly available, let me summarize them briefly here. The same young woman appears in a number of them. She is in fact the only person we see, except for a bullfighter, whose images dominate three of the ten pages, dressed in his splendid costume, the brilliant, glittering "suit of lights." In the first of the ten pages the woman is part of a photomontage in which several images are printed together, so that we cannot tell exactly where she is or what we are seeing. She is partly clothed and her hair is disheveled. She appears to be standing, but the image also suggests that she might be lying in a bed. Behind her in the upper half of the page is a white background that might be sheets or newspapers or posters. The lower half of the page is dominated by the intermingled images of what appears to be a wrought-iron balcony and part of a suit of lights. The woman's eyes are open but lowered. Her arms appear to be crossed over her breasts in a protective gesture. In or near her hands is a string of beads, possibly a rosary.

The other pages carry out these motifs in various ways. In one two-page spread the same woman, in a black blouse and wearing shorts decorated on the sides to suggest the embroidery of a suit of lights, lies bent over a low bench or stool, as if to be spanked or whipped. Here she gazes straight into the camera. On another page, with her eyes closed and her lips slightly parted, she seems to swoon against a tattered wall poster of the bullfighter who appears on the other pages. A black shawl or mantilla hangs from her hand, which is pressed against the heart of the bullfighter on the poster. The other pages carry these motifs further. We are given a strong dose here of what Roland Barthes would have called "Latinicity"—that is, certain stereotypes or cultural codes that link things Hispanic with the erotic and the violent, as in Mérimée's or Bizet's *Carmen* and Hemingway's *Death in the Afternoon* or *The Sun Also Rises*. The young woman, with her black hair, her thick, straight eyebrows, her mantilla, and (in two of the pages) her black sombrero, is presented to us as a Hispanic or Latin beauty—though a very well scrubbed and well depilated one, to be sure, as the readers of *Vanity Fair* are presumed to be themselves.

One ad in this sequence combines all these motifs. Our young lady manages to be wearing a white blouse like a schoolgirl, a cummer-bund like a bullfighter (who always wears one under the suit of lights), and a bullfighter's black tie, while holding up a pair of horns in such way as to make her appear like the bull awaiting the sword of the matador with a certain sultry submissiveness—images which recall some of Picasso's late works as well as the literary texts we have mentioned. This female bull has a thing about bullfighters and is clearly waiting there in her striking Guess Jeans jacket for one to come along and put her out of her misery. Her downcast eyes (carefully made up, of course) proclaim her submission, and the dangerous points of those horns are outside the frame of the picture. She is only playing, after all, but you, too, can play if you will join her by encasing your own dangerous attractions in some jeans by Georges Marciano. That is the message—or at least one important message—conveyed by this rich and visually fascinating series of images, which function to make it harder than it ought to be for the reader to avoid going for this bull.

Before concluding this consideration of advertising rhetoric, we should at least glance at the way appraisive-valuative discourse works in a medium that combines the powers and pleasures of speech, visual images, and music. "Glance" is an unfortunate—and therefore reveal-ing—metaphor for what we shall be undertaking, here, since it names precisely what we cannot do in this situation with respect to this kind of text. It is bad enough to discuss magazine advertisements without permission to reprint them, but even harder to discuss a multitrack medium like video in a discourse that is purely verbal. Nevertheless, we must at least consider the rhetoric of video, because it is so power-ful, so ubiquitous in our culture, and because it brings into play the temporal or narrative dimension of evaluative discourse in a very vivid manner. Appealing, as it does, to a wide audience, it will also provide an appropriate occasion to consider the relation of specific texts to the cultural codes against which they must be read.

The moments of surrender proposed to us by video texts come in many forms, but all involve a complex dynamic of power and pleasure. We are, for instance, offered a kind of power through the enhance-ment of our vision. Close-ups position us where we could never stand.

Slow motion allows us an extraordinary penetration into the mechanics of movement, and, combined with music, lends a balletic grace to ordinary forms of locomotion. Filters and other devices cause us to see the world through jaundiced or rose-colored optics, coloring events with emotion more effectively than verbal pathetic fallacy and less obtrusively. These derangements of normal visual processing can be seen as either constraints or extensions of visual power—that is, as power over the viewer or as extensions of the viewer's own optical power, or both. Either way they offer us what is perhaps the greatest single virtue of art: change from the normal, a defense against the ever-present threat of boredom. Video texts, like all except the most utilitarian forms of textuality, are constructed upon a base of boredom, from which they promise us relief.

Visual fascination—and I have mentioned only a few of its obvious forms—is just one of the matrices of power and pleasure that are organized by video texts. Others include narrativity and what I should like to call, at least tentatively, cultural reinforcement. By narrativity, of course, I mean the pleasures and powers associated with the reception of stories presented in video texts. By cultural reinforcement, I mean the process through which video texts confirm viewers in their ideological positions and reassure them as to their membership in a collective cultural body. This function, which operates in the ethical-political realm, is an extremely important element of video textuality and, indeed, an extremely important dimension of all the mass media. This is a function performed throughout much of human history by literature and the other arts, but now, as the arts have become more estranged from their own culture and even opposed to it, the mass media have come to perform this role. What the epic poem did for ancient cultures, the romance for feudalism, and the novel for bourgeois society, the media—and especially television—now do for the commodified, bureaucratized world that is our present environment.

It is time, now, to look at these processes as they operate in some specific texts. Let us begin with a well-known Budweiser commercial, which tells—most frequently in a format of twenty-eight seconds, though a longer version also exists—the life story of a black man pursuing a career as a baseball umpire. In this brief period of time, we are given enough information to construct an entire life story—provided we have the cultural knowledge upon which this construction depends. The story we construct is that of a young man from the provinces, who gets his "big break," his chance to make it in the big city, to rise to the top of his profession. We see him working hard in the small-time, small-town atmosphere of the minor leagues, where the pace of events is slower and more relaxed that it is "at the top." He gets his chance for success—the voice-over narrator says, "In the minors you got to make all the calls, and then one day you *get* the call"—after which we see him face his first real test. He must call an important and "close" play correctly and then withstand the pressure of dispute, neither giving ground by changing his mind (which would be fatal) nor reacting too vigorously to the challenge of his call by an offended manager. His passing of this test and being accepted is presented through a later scene in a bar, in which the manager who had staged the protest "toasts" the umpire with a bottle of Budweiser beer, with a chorus in the background singing, "You keep America working. This Bud's for you." From this scene we conclude that the ump has now "made it" and will live happily ever after. From a few scenes, then, aided by the voice-over narration and a music track, we construct an entire life. How do we do this? We draw upon a storehouse of cultural information that extends from fairy tales and other basic narrative structures to knowledge about the game and business of baseball.

In processing a narrative text we actually construct the story, bringing a vast repertory of cultural knowledge to bear upon the text that we are contemplating. Our pleasure in the narrative is to some extent a constructive pleasure, based upon the sense of accomplishment we achieve by successfully completing this task. By "getting" the story, we prove our competence and demonstrate our membership in a cultural community. And what is the story that we "get"? It is the myth of America itself, of the racial melting pot, of upward mobility, of justice done without fear or favor. The corporate structure of baseball, with minor leagues offering a path for the talented to the celebrity and financial rewards of the majors, embodies values that we all possess, we Americans, as one of the deepest parts of our cultural heritage or ideology. It is, of course, on the playing field that talent triumphs most easily over racial or social barriers. Every year in baseball new faces arrive. Young men, having proved themselves in the minors, get their chance to perform at the highest level. Yale graduates and high-school dropouts who speak little or no English are judged equally by how well they hit, run, throw, and react to game situations. If baseball is still the national pastime, it is because in it our cherished myths materialize—or appear to materialize.

The commercial we are considering is especially interesting because it shows us a black man competing not with his body but with his mind, his judgment and his emotions, in a cruelly testing public arena. Americans who attend to sports are aware that black athletes are just beginning to find acceptance at certain "leadership" positions, such as quarterback in professional football, and that there is still an active scandal over the slender representation of blacks at baseball's managerial and corporate levels. The case of the black umpire reminds viewers of these problems, even as it suggests that here, too, talent will finally prevail. The system works, America works. We can take pride in this. The narrative reduces its story to the absolutely bare essentials, making a career turn, or seem to turn, on a single decision. The ump must make a close call, which will be fiercely contested by a manager who is deliberately testing him. This is a story of initiation, in that respect, an ordeal that the ump must meet successfully. The text ensures that we know this is a test, by showing us the manager plotting in his dugout, and it gives us a manager with one of those baseball faces (Irish? German?) that have the history of the game written on them. This is not just partisan versus impartial judge, it is old man against youth, and white against black. We root for the umpire because we want the system to work—not just baseball but the whole thing: America. For the story to work, of course, the ump must make the right call, and we must know it to be right. Here, the close-up and slow motion come into play—just as they would in a real instant replay—to let us see both how close the call is and that the umpire has indeed made the right call. The runner is out. The manager's charge from the dugout is classic baseball protest, and the ump's self-control and slow walk away from the angry manager are gestures in a ritual we all know. That's right, we think, that's the way it's done. We know these moves the way the contemporaries of Aeschylus and Sophocles knew the myths upon which the Greek tragedies were based. Baseball is already a ritual, and a ritual we partake of mostly through the medium of television. The commercial has only to organize these images in a certain way to create a powerful narrative.

At the bar after the game, we are off stage, outside that ritual of baseball, but we are still in the world of myth. The manager salutes the ump with his tilted bottle of beer; the old man acknowledges that youth has passed its test. The sword on the shoulder of knighthood, the laying on of hands, the tilted Bud—all these are ritual gestures in the same narrative structure of initiation. To the extent that we have wanted this to happen we are gratified by this closing scene of the narrative text, and many things, as I have suggested, conspire to make us want this ending. We are dealing with an archetypal narrative that has been adjusted for maximum effect within a particular political and social context, and all this has been deployed with a technical skill in casting, directing, acting, photographing, and editing that is of a high order. It is very hard to resist the pleasure of this text, and we cannot accept the pleasure without, for the bewildering minute at least, also accepting the ideology that is so richly and closely entangled with the story that we construct from the video text. To accept the pleasure of this text is to believe that America works; and this is a comforting belief, itself a pleasure of an even higher order—for as long as we can maintain it. Does the text also sell Budweiser? This is something only market research (if you believe it) can tell. But it surely sells the American way first and then seeks to sell its brand of beer by establishing a metonymic connection between the product and the nation: a national beer for the national pastime.

An audience that can understand this commercial, successfully constructing the ump's story from the scenes represented in the text and the comments of the narrative voice, is an audience that understands narrative structure and has a significant amount of cultural knowledge as well, including both data (how baseball leagues are organized, for instance, and how the game is played) and myth (what constitutes success, for example, and what initiation is). At a time when critics such as William Bennett and E. D. Hirsch are bewailing our ignorance of culture, it is important to realize that many Americans are not without culture; they simply have a different culture from that of Bennett and Hirsch. What they really lack, for the most part, is any way of analyzing and criticizing the power of a text like the Budweiser commercial—not its power to sell beer, which is easily resisted, especially once you have tasted better beer—but its power to sell America. For the sort of analysis that I am suggesting, it is necessary to recover (as Eliot says) from the surrender to this text, and it is also necessary to have the tools of ideological criticism. Recovery, in fact, may depend upon critical analysis, which is why the analysis of video texts needs to be taught in all our schools.

Before moving on to the consideration of a more complex textual economy; we would do well to pause and consider the necessity of ideological criticism. One dimension of the conservative agenda for this country has been conspicuously anticritical. The proposals of William Bennett and E. D. Hirsch, for instance, different as they are in certain respects, are both recipes for the indoctrination of young people in certain cultural myths. The great books of past ages, in the eyes of Bennett, Hirsch, and Allan Bloom, are to be mythologized, turned into frozen monuments of Greatness in which our "cultural heritage" is embodied. This is precisely what Bloom does to Plato, for instance, turning the dialectical search for truth into a fixed recipe for "greatness of soul." The irony of this is that Plato can only die in this process. Plato's work can better be kept alive in our time by such irreverent critiques as that of Jacques Derrida, who takes Plato seriously as an opponent, which is to say, takes him dialectically. In this age of massive manipulation and disinformation, criticism is the only way we have of taking something seriously. The greatest patriots in our time will be those who explore our ideology critically, with particular attention to the gaps between mythology and practice. Above all, we must start with our most beloved icons, not the ones we profess allegiance to, but those that really have the power to move and shake us. I propose to conclude this discussion by examining such an icon, as it existed for my own generation, across the media of film, radio, phonograph, and television. More current icons I shall prudently

leave to more current investigators. Each generation has its own work
to do.

The right way to consider this icon is to begin by seeing it on
television, but, once again, we are up against the limitations of this
printed medium. Perhaps you have seen it already. I shall hope for
that, while doing as much as I can to compensate for the absence of the
video text. What I am going to discuss is a tape of Judy Garland,
singing "Over the Rainbow" at a stage concert late in her troubled
life. The first time I saw this video, which, as it happens, was not so
very long ago, I found myself experiencing an extraordinarily bewildering minute, moved more deeply—and, as it turns out, further—than I could readily account for. My "recovery" from this
event, to use Eliot's term, was effected through a process of critical
analysis that is now embodied in this text. I present it here in hopes
that my own experience is sufficiently typical to be of some worth as
an example, while also hoping, of course, that my critical analysis will
be sufficiently developed to transcend that typical experience—to be,
in fact, critical. I shall begin by offering a description of the video text
itself.

From its opening moment, this text is not a single or simple entity—in time, space, or emotional register. The first voice we hear is
that of Liza Minelli, telling us that we are about to watch a rare
recording of her mother, Judy Garland (who is now, of course, long
dead) singing in concert the song through which she first became an
icon to the American public, "Over the Rainbow." We then see Judy
Garland, dressed in a tramp costume that she used in the previous
number of her routine. She comes downstage, to sit close to the
audience, and the camera moves in to meet her. As she sings the song,
she begins to weep, at times appearing barely able to continue singing, and her voice, always highly emotional, seems on certain notes
almost a cry of pain. The tramp makeup, with its heavily blackened
and smudged face, gives Garland the appearance of a street urchin at
times, while at other moments she shows her age. The image becomes, for the knowledgeable viewer, a tissue of distinct but related
times: our own viewing time, the time of Minelli's narration, which is
after her mother's death, the time of the recording, with its distance

from us and its authenticity signified by the black-and-white photography itself, and all the other times we have seen or heard Judy Garland sing this song, especially the first time we saw her singing it for the first time (first time for us and first time for her) in the film *The Wizard of Oz*. This collection of moments—of which we as viewers are aware, though how consciously may vary from one person to another—these separate moments catch up in their net the time that has passed between one and another. We are aware, then, at some level, of the difference between ourselves as we were when we first saw Judy Garland singing this song, and, because she has existed as a celebrity in this culture, we are aware of the story of her life as it has entered our cultural awareness, becoming a mythic narrative of the unhappiness of the successful: a story of debauchery and dissolution. Many of us, viewers of her own generation, will remember images of her from other films, seeing her, for instance, as the bloated and faded image of defeated Germany in *Judgment at Nuremberg*, and having seen, in that image, her own life's defeat and dissolution, the abuse of alcohol and barbiturates that, our cultural mythology tells us, led to her early death.

This past, I am arguing, weighs upon us as we watch her singing this song, and it is a double past: her life, as we know it from the popular media, and our own lives, as we have constructed them in our own video of memory. It is because we cannot see her, now, without remembering her, then, that we cannot escape remembering ourselves, then, at the moment of our present viewing. This video text, by its inexorable emotional and temporal logic, forces us to take account of the years between its two major moments. We are thus led to be aware of our lives as lived in time, and, beyond this, we become aware of the difference between the way we are now and—not only the way we were then but also—the way that we thought then that we might be now. Our own former hopes and dreams are evoked by this video text, as we ineluctably narratize the material presented to us. Given so many spots of time, we have no choice but to connect them in two parallel narratives, hers and ours. All this is, of course, enhanced by the subject matter of the song, though the song expresses the same distances through metaphors of space rather than time: the difference

between being here and there; in this place and that other place, over
the rainbow; the difference, as the film textualizes it, between Kansas
and Oz.

In *The Wizard of Oz*, Dorothy sings this song early, while she is still
in Kansas, and she sings it without tears. The film positions the song
as a childish wish for a richer, fuller life, a utopian vision which the
cinematic narrative betrays by treating the whole trip to Oz as the
product of a delirious dream brought on by the concussion that Dorothy sustains during the tornado. The film, in marked contrast to the
novel upon which it was based, rationalizes the fantastic and uses it to
force Dorothy to accept the reality principle. Oz, not history, becomes the nightmare from which Dorothy needs to escape. Given
this, it is interesting that Judy Garland's public has always interpreted
her life as the story of a girl for whom reality was not enough—as the
description of her funeral by Mel Tormé illustrates:

> There were no hysterically shrieking women [as there were at Valentino's
> funeral], but many people in the long queue wept unashamedly as they
> filed past the girl-woman lying in state inside Campbell's. On leaving the
> parlor, one middle-aged lady dabbed at tear-streaked cheeks with a piece of
> Kleenex and intoned, "Well, she's found that rainbow now." [Tormé, vii]

People living lives well this side of the rainbow, who would not trade
them for the disaster that was Judy Garland's life, nevertheless found
in that life an admirable myth of rejection, of refusal to accept what we
all accept in the way of life in this country at this time. It is this myth,
already present in the consciousness of many viewers, that becomes
the source of power for the video image of Judy, the girl-woman,
singing this song about an alternate universe about which we learn no
single physical detail.

It is worth noting, if only in passing, that Dorothy's song is, in its
sentiments, strikingly close to a more complex piece of music, sung by
another trapped young woman, in another country:

Stridono lassù,
liberamente lanciati a vol,
a vol come frecci, gli augel.
Disfidano le nubi e sol cocente,

e vanno, e vanno per le vie del ciel. . . .
Vanno lagggiù, verso un paese strano
che sognan forse e che cercano invan.

They cry out up above,
freely launched in flight,
flying like arrows, the birds.
They challenge the clouds and the blazing sun,
and they travel, they travel along the roads of the sky. . . .
They travel far off, toward a strange land
that perhaps they dreamed and seek in vain.

[Ruggero Leoncavallo, *I Pagliacci*, Act 1]

These are lines from Nedda's song, in act 1 of *I Pagliacci*, as she dreams of escaping from her oppressively jealous husband, and they should remind us here, especially if we can remember the song's haunting melody, that the emotion they arouse in the viewer is rooted in the life and situation of the fictional character, while the emotion generated by Judy Garland singing "Over the Rainbow" on stage is generated by the fiction of her life. Both of these fictions, we should remember, are the creations of the viewers, though grounded in different texts. The opera is relevant here in many ways, because it is an opera about the mixture of life and theatre, with an audience on stage applauding the realism of acting generated by a clown who is genuinely bent upon murdering his wife. Judy Garland, we should remember, liked to perform "Over the Rainbow" still wearing the clownish tramp's costume she used for the preceding song. The makeup, which makes her look like one of those sentimental pictures of kids with enormous eyes, so dear to the heart of gift-shop owners, also functions—because it is makeup for a previous song—to remind us that it is, in fact, makeup—that we are watching an actress. The makeup thus becomes, paradoxically, a sign, an index of Garland's life, since a singing actress is what she *is*. I am suggesting that the interpenetration of art and life upon which the affect of this song depends is not simply gratuitous but is part of the act that Garland developed, an act that included her life. Just as in the opera Nedda's husband, Canio, must laugh while his heart is breaking, Judy Garland must sometimes have wept while her heart jumped for joy. What her audience took to be life breaking in upon art, the real penetrating into the unreal, was in fact itself part of the rhetoric of her performance—which is not, however, to say that such rhetoric is invented ex nihilo. The life that she is using, textualized by film magazines and scandal sheets, is nevertheless a life she lived. Not only is there no perfect separation between rhetoric and art, there is none between life as textualized and life as lived, either. This perverse thesis (as you may find it) is borne out by Mel Tormé's account of seeing Garland perform the song at the Palace Theatre in 1951. He saw her once and went backstage to congratulate her. When he said he wanted to come a second time she tried to discourage him. Here (in abridged form) is his account of both visits:

The moment Garland stepped onto the stage and proceeded to dazzle the packed house with "Swanee," "Rock-a-bye Your Baby," "San Francisco" and the myriad other Garland classics, I finally knew what everyone had been shouting about. And the final pin-dropping moments when she sat, in the tramp costume on the edge of the stage, legs dangling over, lighted only by a single spotlight, and sang "Over the Rainbow" was for me, and everyone else, one of the few really great pieces of theater we would ever see.

. . . .

Two weeks later I returned to the Palace. The reception and attendant ovation for her was, if anything, greater than on the previous occasion. But I saw what she meant [in urging him not to see it again]. I wasn't really disappointed, but having reacted to the first performance on a purely sensory basis, I was now inured enough to examine her act technically. When she sang "Over the Rainbow," the tears rolled down her cheeks at the precise moment they had flowed the last time I had seen her. Later, in her dressing room, she said, "You were surprised when I cried 'on cue' in 'Rainbow,' weren't you? Now admit it, bub, you were surprised and disappointed."

"Like hell I was," I countered. "It just reaffirmed what I already knew; you're not only one hell of a singer, you're a tremendous actress."

"I know," she added, without a drop of conceit, merely acknowledging a proven fact. "But sometimes when I turn the tears on, people who have seen me here before go away disappointed." [Tormé, 12–14]

Mel Tormé experienced the bewildering moment of surrender and only recovered on his second viewing. At that point he could become critical, but only in a "technical" way, as one actor to another. He does not raise the question of what we exchange for our emotional pleasure in this performance. For him the emotional effect is an end in itself. But we must raise the question and shall return to it, after attending to one or two other matters. Not everyone, of course, responds to the Budweiser commercial or to Judy Garland in the manner that I have indicated. I showed these video texts to some visitors from Germany and found that they could scarcely follow the outline of the story of the black umpire and did not really know what had happened. Certainly, they did not feel any surge of American patriotism in watching that little tale. Nor were they moved by Judy Garland. One of them thought that Garland seemed to be having lung trouble, not even recognizing that the famous tears were supposed to be signs of sorrow or suffering. Watching them watch "Over the Rainbow" was like watching Martians observe a couple of Earthlings making love. They found the emotion absurd and forced, to the extent that they noticed that it was present at all. They were, in fact, scarcely engaged by either of the two video texts that they looked at for me, because they could bring to neither the cultural information that was required to complete the texts in a fashion commensurate with the words, images, and music presented.

Part of my point here is that both texts engage only those readers who share the requisite cultural information. Another part is that these two apparently different texts—one clearly "advertising" and the other just as clearly "art" or "entertainment"—are both thoroughly rhetorical in that they are sites where pleasure and power are interchanged. In the case of the Budweiser commercial, we noted that we exchange our pleasure in that narrative for a share of the American dream, for a cultural reinforcement that is also pleasurable. What we give up, at least until we recover, is the ability to take an imaginative stand outside that dream and to criticize it. This we can accomplish only by the active labor of thought, comparing the textual narrative with information from other sources, including our own experience. Such an achievement of critical thought carries its own power and pleasure, of course, but we obtain these only by consciously putting aside the pleasure of the text and its attendant narrative.

In the case of Garland, the process is similar. We read the performance of "Over the Rainbow" as a scene in a double narrative, the story of Judy Garland's life and that of our own. We are pleased by her tears because they are authenticated by the myth of the unhappy and doomed celebrity, which makes our own failures and frustrations pale in comparison. As we watch her, we think that she is in so much mental anguish that she can barely sing; she almost fails to entertain at all. Her failures clothe her and give a kind of authentication to her tramp's attire and makeup: an authentication that is at once spurious and ultimate. On the one hand, she is acting. She does this on cue, performance after performance. On the other hand, we have her life story, ending in the ultimate authentication, her messy, quasi-suicidal death. We scarcely need Theodor Adorno to remind us that she has packaged her life in order to present it to us as the ultimate commodity in a world that reifies and commodifies everything. This, too, is a rhetoric, but whether it is the ultimate betrayal of art or a mode of art as authentic as any other in this culture, it is impossible—for me, at least—to say. To "recover" from the power of this rhetoric is, on the one hand, as easy as the method of Mel Tormé—we need only see a second performance—and, on the other, it is as hard as imagining the authenticity that may lie on the other side of the rhetorical rainbow itself.

That unimaginable authenticity would be some absolute upon which we might ground our ethics or locate the fulcrum of our Archimedean critical analysis. In such a place we might find the guarantee for Derridean rigor, or the talisman that would enable us to distinguish poetry from propaganda or advertising. On this side of the rainbow, however, we shall have to face the fact that poetry and advertising are both rhetorical genres, so similar in their semiotic texture that they cannot be distinguished on the level of texture alone. If they are to be distinguished, this must be done by going outside the individual texts and beyond their textual media, into the world around them. Dickinson, after all, is not trying to sell us any bird we may actually buy, nor Oliver any particular whale. Even Whitman is not just singing his own body, nor MacLeish his own poetry, though neither Whitman nor MacLeish quite escapes self-promotion. In another sense, of course, no poem escapes self-promotion. Every poem wants to be loved for its own verbal body and not for whatever message it conveys. Much advertising, I would say, has the same division of allegiance. The Budweiser commercial wants to sell beer, to be sure, but it also wants to reaffirm certain ethical-political values, and it wants to be perceived as a well-made object that is aesthetically pleasing for its own sake. What I am suggesting is that the mere fact that advertising rests on hopes that we will rush right out and buy a particular product is not enough to distinguish it from either propaganda or poetry nor to separate the ethical from the unethical in advertising. After all advertising often urges us to do good deeds, just as it often urges us to behave foolishly. A theory of rhetoric will help us decide whether a text is well or ill made but it will not tell us whether what a text advocates is a good or bad end. Rhetoric will help us follow the exchanges of pleasure and power in any textual situation. It will not tell us whether these exchanges are right or wrong. What will?

I have no snappy answer to that question. I have been following Derrida's usage in speaking of the "ethical-political" as a hyphenated notion. It is perhaps time to say clearly why I think this is proper. Earlier we saw that feminism is a rhetoric that draws its strength from a politics, a class-consciousness. But this politics, like all politics, I would argue, depends upon ethical concepts for its legitimation: concepts like justice or fairness, for instance. It is justice, or the belief that equal things should be treated equally, to which feminists must appeal in order to turn their politics into a rhetoric. But justice cannot be done, cannot enter the world of human actions, without becoming political, any more than justice can be put into words or other signs without becoming rhetorical. This need not mean that there are no ethical absolutes. As I pointed out in the previous chapter, for instance, even Derridean deconstruction depends upon a concept like "rigor," which has a whiff of the absolute about it. It does mean, however, as Plato also argued, that we have no direct access to any absolute. The dialectic may help us expose the false and the bad, but it cannot speak the good and the true adequately. Since Hegel, of course, we have had to face the further complication that our textuality is so inexorably conditioned by historical change that our best versions of the ethical and the political lose their efficacy over time and must be reinscribed.

In the next section of this chapter, I shall try to pose this problem of the historicity and textuality of ethics in terms of the historicity of a literary genre: the novel. I have chosen the novel because its life as a literary form or genre has been interestingly intertwined with a particular form of ethical-political textuality—which I shall call Protestantism, a term that will obviously require some definition. The notion of Protestantism that I am using will be elaborated as we go along, but let me offer some preliminary bearings on the topic at once. I mean by *Protestantism* more the spirit that informed the Reformation than any particular sect in which the ideals of the Reformation were embodied or any particular doctrine in which they were codified. Part of what I mean is what Ruskin called "Northern" in his discussion of European cultural tendencies in *The Stones of Venice*:

Strength of will, independence of character, resoluteness of purpose, impatience of undue control, and that general tendency to set the individual reason against authority, and the individual deed against destiny, which, in the Northern tribes, has opposed itself throughout all ages to the languid submission, in the Southern, of thought to tradition, and purpose to fatality. [Ruskin, 175]

As a person in whom Northern and Southern heritage is mixed, let me hasten to say that I do not subscribe to Ruskin's view of the Southern European character; nevertheless, what I mean by *Protestant* is partly encompassed by his definition of Northern qualities. I mean primarily an insistence on the importance of the individual conscience—an insistence derived from the Christian notion of soul as it was modified during the Reformation. This attitude, which was certainly to be found among groups who did not identify themselves as members of any Protestant sect, is nevertheless typified by the beliefs of many such sects. Moreover, during the nineteenth century in particular, this attitude played a dominant role in the culture of Europe—as Hegel argues in *The Philosophy of History*, section III, chapters 1 and 2—helping to shape economic and political life as well as the literary genre we call the novel. Our topic, let us remember, is the relationship of this genre, in its historicity, to ethics. We can begin with some thoughts on the novel as a genre.

Just as every animal belongs to a species, every literary work belongs to a genre. A literary genre, the same as a zoological species, means a certain stock of possibilities. It is erroneous to think of the novel—and I refer to the modern novel in particular—as of an endless field capable of rendering ever new forms. Rather it may be compared to a vast but finite quarry. There exist a definite number of possible themes for the novel. The workman of the primal hour had no trouble finding new blocks—new characters, new themes. But present-day writers face the fact that only narrow and concealed veins are left them. Not only is the difficulty of finding new subjects steadily growing, but ever "newer" and more extraordinary ones are needed to impress the reader. This is the second cause of the difficulty with which the genre as such is faced in our time. Proof that the present decline is due to more fundamental causes than a possibly inferior quality of contemporary novels is given by the fact that, as it becomes more difficult to write novels, the famous old or classical ones appear less good. Only a few have escaped drowning in the reader's boredom.

At this point I must stop and confess to an unethical act. Every word of the previous paragraph has been plagiarized from an essay written sixty years ago by José Ortega y Gasset, called "Notes on the Novel" (58–60). I have done this both in order to raise certain questions about the novel as a literary form and as a way of making concrete the question of how ethics enters textuality. To begin with the latter of these two questions, we should note the way in which, by acknowledging my plagiarism and naming the source of the formerly plagiarized words, I have transformed an unethical act into an ethical one. What began as theft has ended as the quotation and citation of authority. The unethical has become the ethical by the uttering of a few additional words which have served to invoke what we might call an ethical code—a code situated outside my utterance, in a cultural space, in this case that of a certain academic or professional discourse, which supports and enables my particular practice. If we are to consider the relationship between any specific textual practice and some behavioral paradigm or code that we can call "ethical," a major question will have to be how a particular text, for example this or that fictional narrative, can be connected to a general code of behavior. This question—of the relationship between a narrative text and some ethical system—will serve as our point of departure in this discussion, but before posing it more concretely I should like to return to those provocative statements about the decline of the novel that I stitched together from a few pages of Ortega y Gasset.

It would be absurd to subscribe to what Ortega says in the quoted passage, because he is simply wrong about nearly everything he mentions in it; moreover, his metaphors are careless and inept as well—but I did not quote him to aggrandize myself or contemporary criticism at his expense. I think he is very much alive as a writer, and I believe that in those "Notes on the Novel" he says some things that are both eloquent and important. Consider this, for instance: "The titles of certain books are like the names of cities in which we used to live for a time. They at once bring back a climate, a peculiar smell of streets, a general type of people and a specific rhythm of life" (87). Now that is not only well said; it is also true. And there—even in the passage I plagiarized earlier, and then cited as an authority, and then rejected—even there, in those admittedly inadequate sentences—a perspective on the novel is introduced that we cannot afford to ignore.

Ortega reminds us that literary genres exist in time, that they rise, flourish, and decline, and that the talent of individuals is enhanced or diminished by the possibilities for artistic production that a particular genre makes available at a particular time. He also reminds us that history brings with it a changed perspective on the novels of the past. In 1925 it seemed to him that most of the famous or classical texts in the genre were, in his pungent phrase, "drowning in the reader's boredom." Sixty years or so later, Ortega's sentiments themselves have a "period" flavor, a modernist intolerance that is not at all like our present view, for it is now the case that many people—including academic and professional critics and reviewers—are actually indifferent to the serious art and literature of our own time but take delight in the painting, music, and fiction of the nineteenth century. Ortega, though he might not have anticipated this, can help us understand it:

Let us observe ourselves the moment we have finished reading a great
novel. Is it not as though we were emerging from another world where we
were held incommunicado? That there can have been no communication is
clear; for we were aware of no transition. A second ago we were in Parma
with Count Mosca and La Sanseverina, with Clélia and Fabrice; we lived
their lives with them, immersed in their atmosphere, their time and place.
Now, abruptly we find ourselves in our room, our city, our time; and
already our accustomed preoccupations begin to stir. There is an interval of
indecision and suspense. Perchance a sudden wave of recollection washes
us back into the universe of the novel, and with a certain effort, as though
struggling through a liquid element, we must regain the shores of our
existence proper. Were someone to find us in just that moment, our dilated
pupils would betray our shipwrecked condition. [91]

To read a novel is indeed to dwell in another place, to exchange one's
own horizon for the horizon of the narrative, so that the transition
from the fictional world to actuality may easily leave us momentarily
disoriented. This situation becomes even more complicated and consequential when the "actual" world to which we return causes us to
feel "shipwrecked" or cast away. This metaphor—of "the shores of
our existence proper" to which we must struggle through a "liquid
element" of imagination—becomes even more powerful if we find
our "proper" existence itself an alienating experience.

In proclaiming the exhaustion of the novel as a genre Ortega allowed himself, at least momentarily, to consider the problem in terms
too exclusively formal. A literary genre is *not* like a quarry with only so
much rock in it but is a variable structure that waxes and wanes
through its relationship to other cultural variables. The novel as a
genre has in fact always been linked with certain other cultural phenomena. Like democratic or republican forms of government and the
capitalistic economic system, it has been preeminently the creature of
that form of decadent Christianity known as Protestantism.

I do not mean the word *decadent* as an insult here—anything but. I
think of Protestantism as the fairest flower of Christian thought, with
Deism and Unitarianism as the loveliest petals on that flower, of
which social democracy is the finest fruit. Capitalism, as an economic
system, and the novel, as a literary form or genre, have grown from the

same branch of the same tree. If the novel is in trouble as a form—and I think it is—this is because the culture of enlightened Protestantism is itself in trouble, because capitalism is in trouble, and because social democracy is in trouble, for the ethical code of which the novel has been an expression is precisely that of Protestant capitalist democracy. Thus, if the plight of the novel is a concern, it is not for any purely formal reason. It is because the plight of a cultural heritage and a way of life is a concern.

I am not saying that fiction can no longer be written. It will never stop. Narration is as elemental a feature of human existence as language itself. I am saying only that a particular narrative form—the novel—is so tied to a certain ideology and a certain cultural practice that its life span is indissolubly linked to that ideology and that cultural practice. Nor am I saying that a writer's individual faith will prevent him or her from writing novels within a culture dominated by the Protestant/capitalist/democratic paradigm. One may profess any religion or none at all and still write novels. What counts is the strength of what I am calling the Protestant code within a given cultural situation. In the nineteenth century, for example, the great Russian novelists absorbed this code through their reading of French and English texts, though they lived in a country in which official Protestantism made few inroads. At the present moment, the strength of this code varies from place to place in the world and even within different segments of the population in a single country.

This linkage between a literary form and a cultural or ideological structure is in no way describable in terms of causes in one sphere leading directly to effects in the other. No ideology can generate a perfect transmission of its values—even with a ministry of propaganda established to accomplish that very feat. Nor can any artifact single-handedly bring about a massive cultural change. *Uncle Tom's Cabin*, for instance, had its enormous effect on a certain audience only because that audience had already been constituted by the very Protestant ethical tradition that I have been alluding to as the cultural matrix of the novel. Dante's *Commedia* (to name another powerfully ethical narrative) was not aimed at changing minds but at giving concrete embodiment to what its readers already knew. The novel, on the other hand (as opposed to the epic, romance, and allegory), assumes that consciousness is *defined* by its changeability and that a narrative text should aim at that very dimension of consciousness which is called conscience. Harriet Beecher Stowe did not have to deploy a new ethical code. She had only to make concrete the tension between the practice of slavery and a paradigm already in place for many of her readers, which she did, to powerful ethical-political effect. Even James Joyce, as we saw in chapter 1, when he still saw himself as operating within the tradition of the novel, conceived of that role in terms of generating an ethical code for his people, that is, precisely as a matter of creating a conscience.

As a further illustration of the textualization of ethics in the novel, I should like to turn now, however briefly, to a work which is not only paradigmatically ethical but is the very model and type of everything I have been saying about the relationship between this narrative form and a particular ethical code: George Eliot's *Middlemarch*. I want to discuss *Middlemarch* not only for its many virtues, which led Virginia Woolf to call it "one of the few English novels written for grown-up people" (172), nor simply because Eliot has been regularly charged— as F. R. Leavis ruefully acknowledged—with being "peculiarly addicted to moral preoccupations" (12); I have selected *Middlemarch* as a paradigmatic ethical novel because I can remember vividly my own first reading of it forty years ago—and the ethical shock of finding myself far too closely mirrored in the character of Fred Vincy, who is nicely summed up by the narrator as one of those "young gentlemen whose consciousness is chiefly made up of their own wishes" (89). That, as a dear friend of mine observed upon hearing this confession, "was before you grew up and turned into Casaubon"— an observation that, despite its wickedness and gross inaccuracy of reference, suggests that the book can still function in a normative fashion, as a table of behavioral exemplars to be matched with the names of actual people, who may then be judged according to the ethical values assigned the characters in the novel, who have themselves already been judged and assigned positive or negative ethical weight by the author and narrator of the novel, in terms of that larger pattern of Protestant values to which everything in the book has been referred.

This power of normative ethical discourse is characteristic of the great nineteenth-century novels. In recent years, it has often been discussed in terms of some art of characterization that has been unaccountably rejected or just plain lost by what must clearly be an inferior breed of contemporary writers. Or, in terms such as those suggested by Ortega y Gasset in his "Notes on the Novel," this "decline" in characterization has been attributed to the exhaustion of a vein, all the types of character having already been quarried by previous generations of laborers. I am suggesting, on the contrary, that what is lacking—in both life and art—is not at all a matter of skill or talent or disposition but precisely that sense of consciousness as conscience that is so central to George Eliot's work but so difficult to recapture at our present moment in our thoroughly rhetoricized and sophisticated culture. To be more precise about this it will be necessary to look more closely at the way George Eliot's narrative voice describes the consciousness of characters in the novel. Here are some samples (with emphasis added):

It was not indeed entirely an improvisation, but had taken shape in *inward colloquy*, and rushed out like the round grains from a fruit when sudden heat cracks it. [of Dorothea, 149]

In her indignation there was a sense of superiority, but it went out for the present in firmness of stroke, and did not compress itself into an *inward articulate voice*. [of Dorothea, 209]

Any *inward debate* Lydgate had as to the consequences. . . . [255]

Will Ladislaw on his side felt that his dislike was flourishing at the expense of his gratitude, and spent much *inward discourse* in justifying the dislike. [264]

The Vicar was holding an *inward dialogue*. . . . [299]

"She knows that I know," said *the ever restless voice within*. [of Casaubon, 322]

"There really is nothing to care for much," said poor Rosamond *inwardly*. [439]

He took no notice of it, and went on with an *inward drama and argument*. [of Lydgate, 483]

He *inwardly declared* that he intended to obey orders. [of Bulstrode, 516]

Dorothea, Lydgate, Ladislaw, Farebrother, Casaubon, Rosamond—even Bulstrode—all hear that "ever restless voice within," which is not simply a novelistic device but a conception of character as defined by conscience, in terms of what George Eliot calls inward colloquy, inward articulate voice, inward debate, inward discourse, inward dialogue, and inward drama and argument. Now the notion of inward debate is as old as Homer, but the coupling of it with the Protestant notion of individual conscience is the special domain of the novel, a matter that George Eliot's powerful text clearly illustrates.

This ethical Protestantism is visible everywhere in *Middlemarch*. It is in the dozens—perhaps hundreds—of moments when the narrative voice turns away from a particular occasion or event to make a moral generalization—often by shifting into the first person plural in mid-sentence, as the following examples, which are entirely typical, will illustrate:

Will was not without his intentions to be always generous, but *our* tongues are like little triggers which have usually been pulled before general intentions can be brought to bear. [267, emphasis added]

He [Mr. Brooke] had never been insulted on his own land before and had been inclined to regard himself as a general favorite (*we* are all apt to do so, when *we* think of *our own* amiability more than of what other people are likely to want of *us*). [291, emphasis added]

These invocations of general principles are indispensable to George Eliot as a means—as *the* means—of connecting singular characters and events to the larger ethical field that justifies the writing and reading of novels as a serious matter. But this field is conceived not as some authoritarian code but as the space where conscience plays. The justification for novels, in George Eliot's view, is tied to her suspicion of ethical codes or, as she puts it, "general doctrine," and nowhere is she more the voice of Protestant consciousness than when she criticizes such doctrines: "There is no general doctrine which is not capable of eating out our morality if unchecked by the deep-seated habit of direct fellow-feeling with individual fellow-men" (453). By opposing "morality" to "general doctrine," Eliot takes her stand on quintessentially Protestant ground, and by making "fellow-feeling" for individuals the center of that morality she makes a case for the novel as a major locus in the development of such fellow-feeling. But this passage is not presented directly as a justification for fiction in a serious world, but in another connection entirely, which we should now examine. The narrator is talking about that excellent capitalist, Mr. Bulstrode:

The service he could do to the cause of religion had been through life the ground he alleged to himself for his choice of action: it had been the motive which he had poured out in his prayers. Who would use money and position better than he meant to use them? Who could surpass him in self-abhorrence and exaltation of God's cause? And to Mr. Bulstrode God's cause was something distinct from his own rectitude of conduct: it enforced a discrimination of God's enemies, who were to be used merely as instruments, and whom it would be as well if possible to keep out of money and consequent influence. Also, profitable investments in trades where the power of the prince of this world showed its most active devices, became sanctified by a right application of the profits in the hands of God's servant. This implicit reasoning is essentially no more peculiar to evangelical belief than the use of wide phrases for narrow motives is peculiar to Englishmen. There is no general doctrine which is not capable of eating out our morality if unchecked by the deep-seated habit of direct fellow-feeling with individual fellow-men. But a man who believes in something else than his own greed, has necessarily a conscience or standard to which he more or less adapts himself. [453]

Max Weber's *Protestant Ethic and the Spirit of Capitalism* can be seen as a somewhat belated gloss upon passages like this in *Middlemarch*. Eliot was aware of the close connection between Protestantism and capitalism—and of the complex web of support and contradiction in which they were bound. Her awareness, and its limits, are perhaps most accessible to us in the ethical center of the book: her portrait of Caleb Garth. Garth is presented to us as a man of the highest ethical probity and—what is more important than mere righteousness—of genuine and effective good will. The evolution of the concept of benevolence in the English novel, from Fielding to George Eliot, is a fascinating theme, and far too vast for the present occasion, but we should notice that Caleb Garth's benevolence takes the form of what he himself calls "business," in which the Protestant ethic and the spirit of capitalism are indeed hand in glove. Listen to Garth holding forth on this theme:

"No, no; but it's a fine thing to come to a man when he's seen into the nature of business: to have a chance of getting a bit of the country into good fettle, as they say, and putting men into the right way with their farming, and getting a bit of good contriving and solid building done— that those who are living and those who come after will be the better for. I'd sooner have it than a fortune. I hold it the most honourable work there is. . . . It's a great gift of God, Susan." [295]

"Business" in Caleb Garth's view is doing good, making the world a better place to live, "a great gift of God." Within Garth's speech business is specifically set against the acquisition of a "fortune," though it is clearly seen as creating prosperity for both present and future inhabitants of the country where such good business is done. It is, I should say, capitalism without capital, and once we think of it that way we can see how the entire character of Caleb Garth has been constructed in such a way as to avoid or hide the contradiction between Protestantism and capitalism that lies at the heart of their union. We can observe this best in the extended passage devoted to Caleb's vocation and his character in Book 3:

Caleb Garth often shook his head in meditation on the value, the indispensable might of that myriad-headed, myriad-handed labour by which the social body is fed, clothed, and housed. It laid hold of his imagination in boyhood. The echoes of the great hammer where roof or keel were a-making, the signal shouts of the workmen, the roar of the furnace, the thunder and plash of the engine, were a sublime music to him; the felling and lading of timber, and the huge trunk vibrating star-like in the distance along the highway, the crane at work on the wharf, the piled-up produce in warehouses, the precision and variety of muscular effort wherever exact work had to be turned out,—all these sights of his youth had acted on him as poetry without the aid of the poets, had made a philosophy for him without the aid of philosophers, a religion without the aid of theology. . . .
. . . Though he had never regarded himself as other than an orthodox Christian, and would argue on prevenient grace if the subject were

proposed to him, I think his virtual divinities were good practical schemes, accurate work, and the faithful completion of undertakings: his prince of darkness was a slack workman. But there was no spirit of denial in Caleb, and the world seemed so wondrous to him that he was ready to accept any number of systems, like any number of firmaments, if they did not obviously interfere with the best land-drainage, solid building, correct measuring, and judicious boring (for coal). In fact, he had a reverential soul with a strong practical intelligence. But he could not manage finance: he knew values well, but he had no keenness of imagination for monetary results in the shape of profit and loss: and having ascertained this to his cost, he determined to give up all forms of his beloved "business" which required that talent. [185]

The passage is far too long to be quoted fully here, and I have had to omit much that is of interest, but I think we can see even in this brief excerpt how George Eliot has tried to insulate Caleb Garth from the capitalist side of capitalism by giving him a marvelous talent for what she and he call "business" and no ability at all in the area of finance—which leads to a picture of a man with a keen sense of values but no imagination of profit and loss. As a result, she is able to conclude this portrait by saying that he devoted himself to those kinds of "work which he could do without handling capital."

Contemplating the character of Caleb Garth, one cannot help but feel that the lovableness of the character has been purchased not simply at the expense of his believability but at the cost of the conflict between Christianity and capitalism being put into brackets and dis-posed of—or, in a word, repressed. This particular repression, I should say, constitutes the essence of late Protestantism. In the case of Caleb Garth, it is interestingly correlated with another repression—that of the division of labor, and, in particular, the crucial separation between labor and management, for Caleb Garth's attitude toward rank in the world of business is described as follows: "he thought very well of all ranks but he would not himself have liked to be of any rank in which he had not such close contact with 'business' as to get often honourably decorated with marks of dust and mortar, the damp of the engine, or the sweet soil of the woods and fields." The rhetoric of this passage is fascinating, designed as it is to allow the marks of toil to appear only as badges of honor or decorations—and in that phrase "honourably decorated" we have both valor and frivolity, nicely balanced.

Surely the portrait of Caleb Garth is a miracle of balance—or of the repression of conflicts that threaten the Protestant code itself. Garth is a hero of business but uncontaminated by capital and only "decorated" with the badges of labor. He exists in a pastoral world, forty years before the time of the novel's composition, which suggests that already, in George Eliot's time, the contradictions between the Protestant ethic and its economic concomitant, capitalism, were making themselves felt. *Middlemarch,* unquestionably the greatest work of English realism, was already marked by nostalgia, a repression of its own world's actualities, a repression without which the Protestant code essential to its realization might not have remained viable. Now, a century later, that code lies broken beyond all reconstitution, and both our world and the texts in which we try to speak about that world suffer from our inability to find a viable replacement for it.

My point in reading *Middlemarch* as a textualization of the Protestant ethic has been that all ethical discourses, without exception, are themselves texts and thus are subject to the exigencies of history and rhetoric—and so are literary genres. The fact that we always encounter ethics in some mediated fashion, however, tells us nothing whatsoever about the durability or extent of ethical principles. There is no case, either for relativism or absolutism, to be made from our immersion in textuality. Still, this immersion, or our present awareness of it, may well account for the proliferation of attempts to derive an ethics from textuality itself. The most promising of these, though I cannot begin to discuss it on the present occasion, seems to be the effort of Jürgen Habermas to found an ethical-political system upon an ideal of communication. The least promising, for many reasons, is the attempt of J. Hillis Miller to base an ethics of reading upon the deconstructive literary theory of the late Paul de Man. This attempt, in *The Ethics of Reading,* now stands in an ironic relation to the events of what Jacques Derrida has called "Paul de Man's War," since Miller argues in this book that reading involves a universal necessity to lie. But we must not let the problems of de Man's youthful literary journalism distract us from our more general concern, which is the relationship between ethics and reading. Miller, as we shall see, approaches this matter by situating ethics within reading, seeking to generate an ethic out of reading, an ethic *of* reading.

In his opening chapter, "Reading Doing Reading," Miller argues that in order to be an ethical act, reading cannot be free: "If the response is not one of necessity, grounded in some 'must,' if it is a freedom to do what one likes, for example to make a literary text mean what one likes, then it is not ethical" (4). The problem in this formulation is that it leaves no space between determinism and anarchy. What is missing—between "must" and "what one likes"—is ethics itself, in the form of "ought" or "should." Miller regularly, and I should say deliberately, confounds the necessity to read (something that cannot be avoided) with the obligation to read rightly (something that is avoided all the time). In many respects his version of reading is similar to Milton's version of the fall—only without free will and redemption. It is as if our first parents were presented by God (or Satan, it is not clear which) with a tree of many different fruits and ordered to pick the right one. After they have made their choice, they are then forced to *prove* that it is the right one. Since they cannot do this—not having any direct access to the mind of God (or Whoever)—they are held to have failed, as indeed they were doomed to fail from the start. None of this "sufficient to have stood though free to fall" stuff. Falling is the only option in Miller's deconstructive universe.

Miller also insists that an ethics of reading must not be contaminated by anything outside reading, such as the political or the epistemological—or, we might add, the ethical. Reading must be a pure act: "If there is to be such a thing as an ethical moment in the act of reading, teaching, or writing about literature, it must be sui generis, something individual and particular, itself a source of political or cognitive acts, not subordinated to them" (5). Reading must have its own ethics, an ethics of reading, rather than function within some larger field of values. Miller goes so far as to say that "an ethical act that is fully determined by political considerations or responsibilities is no longer ethical. It could even in a certain sense be said to be amoral" (4). The word *fully* in this statement is an equivocator, since it would be hard to point to any act of reading that is "fully" political or "fully" anything else. Miller does not say how he feels about acts of reading that are "partly" or "mainly" shaped by political considerations, or concerns about gender, or any other questions of value outside of reading itself, but the thrust of his remark, if we ignore the equivocation, is to reinstate the New Critical notion of immanence, of literature as a separate domain, with its own laws and its own ethics. He wants to discredit readings that are interested, tendentious, or based on anything other than a transcendental humanism. This attempt to establish a *cordon sanitaire* around the act of reading will not, in fact, stand up to deconstructive scrutiny, though it is done in the name of deconstruction.

There are other problems as well that emerge when Miller tries to describe this immanent ethic of reading, which he defines as "that aspect of the act of reading in which there is a response to the text that is both necessitated, in the sense that it is a response to an irresistible demand, and free, in the sense that I must take responsibility for my response" (43). This description equivocates about both necessity and freedom. Miller does not say whether the "irresistible demand" simply forces us to make some choice as readers—between this reading and that, for instance—or whether the "irresistible demand" is the necessity of making the right choice. In fact, he rather suggests that it is the necessity of making the wrong choice. This is not simply a failure to be precise. Miller's argument requires this obscurity. He maintains (*a*) that we have no choice but to read, to seek the right reading of the texts around us (and he does, as we shall see, believe that there is one right reading of every text); (*b*) that we can never achieve that right reading; or (*c*) that if we happen to achieve it we will have no way of knowing or verifying that we have achieved it. His treatment of freedom and responsibility suffers from the same problem. He says that what he means by freedom is responsibility—which is odd. Normally we think of freedom as a condition upon which responsibility depends. We do not hold people responsible for what they have done unless they were free to do it. But Miller seems to see things the other way round. If we are held responsible, it must be because we were free. In fact, he never discusses freedom at all and appears to believe that human actions, including reading, are fully determined.

Perhaps the major problem with Miller's discussion is that what he is talking about is not really ethics at all. It is as if he were describing the solution of a problem in mathematics as an ethical matter. There is a right answer, and we have no choice but to seek it. If we get the wrong answer, this is to be considered not a failure in math but an ethical failure, a sort of sin. The only difference between this situation and the situation of reading as Miller describes it is that in reading there are no verifiably right answers, so that one gets it wrong all the time. What Miller is talking about is not mathematics, of course, but it is not ethics, either. It is simply hermeneutics or textual interpretation—plus the consciousness of sin.

In this view the only thing that we can properly call ethical is a response to an absolute demand to act in a certain way, a position that Miller—in a masterpiece of misreading—credits to Kant's categorical imperative. Be that as it may, reading, according to de Man and Miller, always subjects us to such a demand. Specifically, reading requires that we read, but this required reading always results in our failure to read truly. This failure, however, is the very mark of our ethicity (de Man's word), the mark of our having obeyed the law of reading, which requires us to fail. The only way to get it right is to get it wrong, which we cannot help but do. You will think that I am parodying Miller here. If so, compare what I have said to a passage in his own words:

Ethicity is a region of human life in which lying is necessarily made into a universal principle, in the sense that ethical judgments are necessary but never verifiably true. The failure to read or the impossibility of reading is a universal necessity, one moment of which is that potentially aberrant form of language called ethical judgment or prescription. [51]

Let us pause and examine the reasoning of this for a moment. Miller is saying that any statement that cannot be verified must be called a lie. In other words, he is suppressing the distinction between utterances that are intentionally deceitful—to which we normally apply the word *lie*—and utterances that simply cannot be tested for truth value—whether or not they are accompanied by any intention to deceive and regardless of whether they may happen to be true. This is the sort of thinking that gave Sophistry a bad name. Miller also appears to believe that nothing that is textual can be tested for truth value. If he believes that, I wonder what he thinks Derrida is doing when he responds to Habermas's critique of his work by saying, "That is false. I say *false*, as opposed to *true*" (*Limited Inc*, 157). Does Miller think Derrida is lying here? Does he consider Derrida's statements and Habermas's statements equally untruthful? And where can this notion of the "verifiably true" come from? Science? Logic? Positivism? If truth is impossible and everyone must lie all the time, then the concepts of truth and lies are empty, useless. Why, then, does Miller continue to use them? He uses them, in a move that should be familiar to us now, as a way of generating deconstructive pathos for rhetorical effect. He wants to shock us with his assertion that we are all necessarily liars, and he wants to shame us with the possibility of verifiable truth all the same. This is what Hegel, contemptuously using the French word, called *raisonnement*. But it is as far from being reasonable as it is from being ethical. Miller is defining ethics as being beyond right and wrong. He also defines it as being beyond human choice:

An act of reading, moreover, takes place as something which is bound to happen as it does happen, to a certain person in a certain psychological, interpersonal, historical, political, and institutional situation. . . .

Readings that "take place" in this way are "true" in the special sense of being true to an implacable law of language, that is, the law of the failure to read, not truth of correspondence to some transcendent and universal Truth with a capital T. [53]

There is only one right reading, but there are many readers. And each reader is unique—"a certain person in a certain . . . situation." Since only one reading can be right, and since every reading must be different from all the other readings, the number of wrong readings must be infinity minus one. That's a lot of error—but the whole equation stands or falls on the correctness of its postulate that there is and ought to be only one right reading. My most persistent reaction to this kind of "cleverness" is to say that there ought to be an implacable law forbidding literary critics to dabble in philosophy. This line of thought reduces ethics to necessity and eliminates choice altogether, making the reader a totally passive victim of the law. Instead of "Truth with a capital T" we are given Law with a capital L. Not only do I fail to see the gain in this exchange, I fail to see the difference. What Miller offers us instead of truth is a deterministic nightmare from which we can never awaken:

> To live is to read, or rather to commit again and again the failure to read which is the human lot. We are hard at work trying to fulfill the impossible task of reading from the moment we are born until the moment we die. We struggle to read from the moment we wake in the morning until the moment we fall asleep at night, and what are our dreams but more lessons in the pain of the impossibility of reading, or rather the pain of having no way of knowing whether or not we may have in our discursive wanderings and aberrancies stumbled by accident on the right reading? Far from being "indeterminate" or "nihilistic," however, or a matter of wanton free play or arbitrary choice, each reading is, strictly speaking, ethical, in the sense that is *has* to take place, by an implacable necessity, as the response to a categorical demand, and in the sense that the reader *must* take responsibility for it and for its consequences in the personal, social, and political worlds. [59]

I love the puritanical violence of this language. *Sinners in the Hands of an Angry Text*! But I don't believe it for a minute. For someone who thinks that "it is impossible to get outside the limits of language by means of language" (59), Miller is far too quick to invoke implacable laws that compel people to the unbearable agonies of reading—as he has defined them. How did he get outside of language to discover these laws? How did he verify them? He insists on the notion of a perfectly complete and accurate reading of every text as a standard by which to judge readings that are by necessity inaccurate or incomplete—and then tantalizes us with the possibility that we might have achieved the ideal reading without knowing it, despite the implacable law that prevents us from doing this very thing. He needs this ideal of "right" reading in order to assert that all our other readings are wrong, that is, in order to make us feel the burden of our hideous fallibility. But this very ideal of a right reading is denied by all the philosophy upon which he bases his literary theory. Texts and people do not abide in some timeless moment but in time. They are both thoroughly impregnated with time; they are constructed and deconstructed in time and by time. They are made of time. And nothing made of time and functioning in time can be complete or perfect. There is no way a human being can stumble upon the right reading by accident, because the right reading is not *there* in human time to be stumbled upon, nor is it sitting unchanged in some heaven of ideal readings. Readings must change. That is what philosophers from Hegel to Heidegger have taught Derrida and the rest of us—and why Miller has not learned it I cannot imagine. But this return to Kant for the foundation of his ethic of reading—doing considerable violence to the old philosopher in the process—is a clear signal that Miller is ignoring the post-Kantian thought that is the necessary basis for deconstruction.

Not to put too fine a point on it, I think this is a perverse notion of reading. It is perverse because in it Miller takes the inevitably centrifugal activity of reading and treats this as if it were a sin, instead of seeing the unfinished, expanding nature of reading as a blessing for both the reader and the text. It is perverse, also, because he treats the centripetal activity of interpretation as a superhuman task that humans are nonetheless compelled to perform, instead of an obligation, in the truly Kantian sense, to read as we would like to be read ourselves and as we would wish everyone to read. And it is especially perverse because he takes the ethical activity of criticism and reduces it to the hermeneutic issue of interpretation, which he then calls "the ethics of reading." In this manner he avoids the ethical-political realm entirely, as if reading had nothing to do with choices and actions involving other human beings. He seems to have forgotten that though we read our culture and our lives as we read books, we also act in our culture and our life as we do not in books. No matter how strongly we feel about Bulstrode, Casaubon, Dorothea Brooke, or any other character in *Middlemarch*, we cannot act in that world. We can only read, interpret, and criticize. When we connect the text of the book to the text of our lives, however, the world of choice and action opens before us. To read about Fred Vincy, to be critical of his behavior, and then to see a resemblance between him and oneself—this is only the beginning of ethics, but it is ethical precisely because it is not forced upon us, not specifically anticipated or required by Eliot's text, nor by any implacable law of reading.

To read in this way—which I would call ethical—the reader must bring the text of Vincy and the text of his life together in a metaphorical connection. This is the basic centrifugal activity of reading as a constructive, creative process. The analogy between Vincy and myself may rise, unbidden, into my consciousness, but then it must be held by an act of will and written into the new text that I am constructing. That is, I must freely accept the character Vincy as a metaphor for myself if this reading is to become ethical—and then I must seek to change my behavior so as to eliminate, or at least reduce, the validity of that metaphor in my life as it continues. For any of this to be possible, of course, it must be assumed that I have some power to change my life, that—to some extent—I am free and therefore responsible. The word *ethics* is a mockery in a world where people are assumed to be totally without freedom and reasonableness, where they never get to choose and can never get things right but must suffer for their inevitable errors—and where the question of the relationship between reading and any form of action beyond discussing one's readings is never even raised.

In the case of American literary critics—such as Jonathan Culler, J. Hillis Miller, and, of course, myself—who have learned much from the French, an opportunity for ethical reading opens when we come upon a passage in *Middlemarch* such as the following:

> In warming himself at French social theories he had brought away no smell of scorching. We may handle even extreme opinions with impunity while our furniture, our dinner-giving, and preference for armorial bearings in our own case, link us indissolubly with the established order. [255]

Eliot is talking about the social theories that led to the French Revolution and not about what we might call the textual revolution of the last few decades, but a reader would have to be ethically obtuse not to see the possibility of extending the applicability of her words to our contemporary situation. She is talking, among other things, about integrity and hypocrisy, about the difference between professing ideas and living by them, accepting their consequences in our own lives. What an American deconstructionist or semiotician faced with this passage ought to do is to ask whether these words may not inscribe him in Eliot's text. Does this shoe fit me? Do I live as if I had fully accepted the implications of whatever French theories I may profess? That is what I ought to think about this passage—not because Eliot anticipated me as her reader but because she has described a sort of ethical weakness that may well be my own. To read critically, and that is what this chapter is about, is to see the blind spots in Eliot's text, as in the portrait of Caleb Garth that I discussed above. But it is also a matter of paying attention when Eliot's text points to what may be a blind spot of my own, or of any other critic who has "warmed himself at French . . . theories."

In his own reading of Eliot's *Adam Bede* in *The Ethics of Reading*, Miller seeks to demonstrate that we cannot, in fact, make ethical judgments about the characters and actions in that novel—that we cannot, for instance, decide "whether Adam's deluded love for Hetty is a good thing or a bad thing" (80). The ground has shifted here from the ethics of reading to the reading of ethics, but even so, what Miller is doing is trivializing the notion of ethics by reducing it to a simple choice between good and bad on a matter that is not really an ethical issue in the first place. Loving someone is not a question of ethics, precisely because we are not free to determine where we love. But what we do about whatever love we may feel is indeed ethical, because we have some choice about what we do. And I imagine that Adam himself would understand this very well. Miller also argues that we never know whether the voice that addresses us in the novel belongs to Mary Ann Evans or to an invented male narrator called George Eliot. "It is both," he says, "and so neither." This sort of statement sounds more plausible than it is. If I have an apple and an orange—both—this does not mean that I really have neither. One plus one does not equal zero, nor does *x* plus *y*. Logic is not Miller's strong point. Neither, as we have seen, is ethics. What he is good at is pathos. He is a master of the peculiar pathos that emerges when we set the deconstructive view of unlimited textuality against our nostalgia for some "lost" ideal of perfect interpretation. By such means he turns the pleasure of the text into pain, a puritanical sort of pain that is, of course, pleasurable in the end because it is fully textual itself, which is to say thoroughly intertextual. This is the pathos of deconstruction, which depends upon situating the reader between a categorical imperative that urges success in reading and an inexorable law that requires failure. This is rhetorically powerful, but it leaves no room for ethics, which requires both freedom and judgment. An ethic of reading can begin only when we are willing to accept some readings as better than others and to say why this is so and to accept some texts as better than others and say why this is so, as I am doing now in the case of Miller himself. Such judgments, it should now be clear, require us to connect what is represented in the text with what we see in the world—in a manner that is ethical because it is political, and political because it is textual. This is a crucial point. The notion of textuality reminds us that we do nothing in isolation from others. We are always connected, woven together, textualized—and therefore politicized. This is why there can be no ethics of reading that is free of political concerns.

To have an ethics means to have standards, canons, protocols. To express these in textual form is—inevitably—to subject them to the exigencies of rhetoric and the vicissitudes of interpretation: to subject them to the whole regime of temporality and textuality. Even to think these protocols, to imagine them, to intuit them, to construct them, is to textualize them. What we can express in the realm of ethics will inevitably be provisional, fully caught up in a historical dialectic that is not guaranteed by any teleology of the absolute to which we can claim access. This does not mean, however, that we inevitably fall into some pathos of unhappy consciousness. It only means that we must build our protocols even as we build our readings, our interpretations, and our criticisms. If we have no Truth with a capital *T*, we must stop using the notion of such Truth—in whatever guise—to measure what we then take to be our failure to attain it. But we must not give up distinguishing between truth and lies within whatever frameworks we can construct to make such determinations. Within such frameworks, some readings are better than others and some texts are better than others, for reasons that we must keep trying to articulate. Finally, of course, though never really finally, we must keep on reading, keep on rewriting the texts that we read in the texts of our lives, and keep on rewriting our lives in the light of those texts.

Works Cited

Aristotle. *The Rhetoric of Aristotle.* Edited by Lane Cooper. Appleton-Century-Crofts, 1960.

Barthes, Roland. "Day by Day with Roland Barthes," pp. 98–117 in Marshall Blonsky, *On Signs.* Johns Hopkins University Press, 1985.

Benveniste, Emile. *Problems in General Linguistics.* University of Miami Press, 1971.

Culler, Jonathan. *On Deconstruction.* Cornell University Press, 1982.

Derrida, Jacques. "But, beyond . . ." *Critical Inquiry* 13:155–70.

———. "Deconstruction in America: An Interview with Jacques Derrida." *Critical Exchange* 17 (Winter 1985): 1–33.

———. *Of Grammatology.* Johns Hopkins University Press, 1967.

———. "The Law of Genre." *Critical Inquiry* 7:55–81.

———. *Limited Inc.* Northwestern University Press, 1988.

———. *Positions.* Translated by Alan Bass. University of Chicago Press, 1981.

———. *Speech and Phenomena.* Northwestern University Press, 1973.

Dilthey, Wilhelm. *Selected Writings.* Edited by H. P. Rickman. Cambridge University Press, 1976.

Eliot, George. *Middlemarch.* Houghton Mifflin, 1956.

Eliot, T. S. *Selected Prose of T. S. Eliot.* Edited by Frank Kermode. Harcourt Brace Jovanovich, 1975.

Ellmann, Richard. *James Joyce.* Oxford University Press, 1959.

Ferrero, Guglielmo. *L'Europa giovane: Studi e viaggi nei paesi del nord.* Garzanti, 1946.

Hegel, G. W. F. *Hegel's Logic* (Part 1 of the *Encyclopaedia*). Oxford University Press, 1975.
————. *The Philosophy of History*. Dover, 1956.
Joyce, James. *Letters*, vol. 2. Edited by Richard Ellmann. Viking, 1966.
————. *Ulysses*. Random House, 1986.
Joyce, Stanislaus. *My Brother's Keeper*. Viking, 1958.
Kermode, Frank. *The Genesis of Secrecy*. Harvard University Press, 1979.
Knapp, Steven, and Walter Benn Michaels. "Against Theory," reprinted pp. 11–30 in W. J. T. Mitchell, ed., *Against Theory*. University of Chicago Press, 1985.
Kolakowski, Leszek. *Husserl and the Search for Certitude*. University of Chicago Press, 1987.
Lawrence, D. H. *The Collected Letters of D. H. Lawrence*. Edited by Harry T. Moore. Viking, 1962.
————. *The Complete Poems of D. H. Lawrence*. Edited by Vivian De Sola Pinto and E. Warren Roberts. Viking, 1964.
————. *Lady Chatterley's Lover*. New American Library, 1962.
————. *Phoenix: The Posthumous Papers of D. H. Lawrence*. Edited by Edward D. McDonald. William Heinemann, 1961.
Leavis, F. R. *The Great Tradition*. Doubleday, 1954.
Leoncavallo, Ruggiero. *I Pagliacci*. Libretto by Guido Menasci and Giovanni Targioni-Tozzetti. Decca Records, 1978.
Lukács, Georg. *Realism in Our Time*. Harper, 1971.
————. *Record of a Life*. Verso, 1983.
————. *Reviews and Articles*. Merlin, 1983.
Merwin, W. S. *The Rain in the Trees*. Alfred A. Knopf, 1988.
Miller, J. Hillis. *The Ethics of Reading*. Columbia University Press, 1987.
Morris, Charles. *Signs, Language, and Behavior*. George Braziller, 1946.
Nietzsche, Friedrich. *The Will to Power*. Random House, 1968.
Oliver, Mary. *American Primitive*. Little, Brown, 1983.
Ortega y Gasset, José. *The Dehumanization of Art and Other Essays on Art, Culture, and Literature*. Princeton University Press, 1968.
Proust, Marcel. *Remembrance of Things Past*, Vol. 2. Translated by C. K. Scott Moncrieff and Frederick A. Blossom. Random House, 1932.
Putnam, Hilary. *Realism and Reason*. Cambridge University Press, 1983.
Rich, Adrienne. *Poems, Selected and New, 1950–1974*. Norton, 1975.
Rorty, Richard. "Deconstruction and Circumvention." *Critical Inquiry* 11:1–23.
————. "the Higher Nominalism in a Nutshell: A Reply to Henry Staten." *Critical Inquiry* 12:462–66.
Rosen, Stanley. *Hermeneutics as Politics*. Oxford University Press, 1987.
Ruskin, John. *The Stones of Venice*. Edited by J. G. Links. Farrar, Straus, and Giroux, 1960.

Russell, Bertrand. *An Inquiry into Meaning and Truth.* Unwin, 1980.

Sanders, Gerald DeWitt, John Herbert Nelson, and M. L. Rosenthal, eds. *Chief Modern Poets of Britain and America.* MacMillan, 1970.

Searle, John R. "Reiterating the Differences: A Reply to Derrida." *Glyph* 1:198–208.

———. "The Word Turned Upside Down." Review of Jonathan Culler's *On Deconstruction.* *New York Review of Books,* 27 October 1983, pp. 74–79.

Skelton, Robin, ed. *Poetry of the Thirties.* Penguin, 1964.

Smith, Dennis Mack. *Mussolini.* Random House, 1982.

Tormé, Mel. *The Other Side of the Rainbow.* William Morrow, 1970.

Valéry, Paul. "Au sujet du 'Cimetière Marin.'" *Nouvelle Revue Française* 40 (1933): 399–411.

Wimsatt, W. K. *The Verbal Icon.* University of Kentucky Press, 1954.

Woolf, Virginia. *The Common Reader.* Harcourt Brace Jovanovich, 1964.

Index